Group Exercises For Enhancing Social Skills and Self-Esteem

SiriNam S. Khalsa

Professional Resource Press
Sarasota, Florida

Published by Professional Resource Press
(An Imprint of Professional Resource Exchange, Inc.)
Post Office Box 15560
Sarasota, FL 34277-1560

The copy editor for this book was Patricia Rockwood, the managing editor was Debbie Fink, the production coordinator was Laurie Girsch, and the cover was created by Carol Tornatore.

Library of Congress Cataloging-in-Publication Data

Khalsa, SiriNam S., date.
    Group exercises for enhancing social skills and self-esteem /
SiriNam S. Khalsa.
        p. cm.
    Includes bibliographical references.
    ISBN: 1-56887-020-5
    1. Social skills--Study and teaching--Activity programs. 2. Self-
esteem--Study and teaching--Activity programs. 3. Group
psychotherapy. I. Title.
HM299.K35 1996
158'.1'07--dc20   96-11493
                                                              CIP

ISBN-13: 978-1-56887-020-5
ISBN-10: 1-56887-020-5

ACKNOWLEDGEMENTS

This book evolved from many years of working with diverse groups of individuals who were striving to improve their chances for succeeding in the "real world." As the exercises presented in this book developed, I was constantly rewarded by the pleasure of working with individuals who were striving to help both themselves and others relate in a more mature and caring fashion.

I cannot possibly acknowledge all of the group participants, mentors, and colleagues whose support helped make this book a reality; however, individual acknowledgements are due to those who most influenced my work and supported the creation of this work.

Thanks to Dr. Larry Ritt and Debra Fink for their editorial and production support in guiding this book to publication, to Kirn Kaur for editing early drafts of this work, and to Nancy Miller for reliably typing the original manuscript. Sincere thank you to Yogi Bahjan, PhD, for his continuing contributions to our understanding of the negative, positive, and neutral minds. Appreciation also to Dr. Joel Levine for his support and the timely humor he displayed during the years we served as co-leaders of social skill groups, and Jack Canfield for his untiring dedication to help others feel good about themselves.

TABLE OF CONTENTS

FOREWORD

For the human service professional, there is perhaps no greater challenge than working with individuals who require enlargement and refinement of emotional adjustment and social skills as part of treatment. People deficient in self-esteem and social skills often confound traditional therapy because of their limitations in prerequisite verbal ability, capacity for insight, and the psychological mindedness required to translate complex internal processes into adequate behavior for intervention. They are also often vulnerable to or victimized by overwhelming social forces.

For these individuals, group process and peer support has been suggested as one avenue the clinician might explore. Self-advocacy and self-help movements such as Alcoholics Anonymous have been cited as examples of group processes that can effect positive growth and change. Problems rooted in low self-esteem such as addiction could, in theory, be better addressed by group advocacy because the problem behaviors and resistance would be more apparent to peers and hence more immediately confronted. The proliferation of self-help and support groups in our culture bears witness to this point of view.

Yet the popularity and power of group processes by themselves offers no guarantee that social skills and self-esteem can be enhanced. Positive client change through *guided group process* is the paramount interest of the clinician and educator, wherein lies the value of the current work before you.

For every self-help group that purports to address the needs of its membership, there are unregulated examples of group process that may lower self-esteem and put clients at risk. Cults and gangs are just the most publicized examples of group process gone wrong. Clinicians are acutely aware that clients who lack social skills and emotional stability are particularly susceptible to the appeal of disabling groups. Dependency and control within an unregulated group context - be it a dysfunctional family or street gang - is a difficulty the human service worker faces in both individual and group treatment.

For therapists and educators interested in harnessing the therapeutic power of guided group process, Mr. Khalsa's collection is a valuable resource. Geared to the needs of clients with self-esteem and social skill deficits, it provides protocols for unlocking and directing the energy potential in groups. To be effective, group work requires the judicious use of sound behavioral principles and carefully designed formats. SiriNam Khalsa has provided a diverse collection of group process exercises that clearly meet this requirement. Carefully thought-out goal statements and sequenced steps for implementation allow the group leader to provide guidance while letting group members take an active role in their own growth.

It is all the more remarkable that, drawing from sources as diverse as humanistic psychology, communication studies, social work, special education, and organizational development, SiriNam Khalsa has been able to format these exercises in a way that group leaders can apply them to participants with low self-esteem and social skill deficits. The collection is eclectic to be sure, and is not meant to be a substitute for clinical training in group work. Yet its value lies in the variety of situations that can be profitably brought to bear on a wide range of group participants' needs, be it ordering food in a restaurant appropriately or identifying human values.

The potential of each exercise to be used as an "ice-breaker" in a therapeutic group or as an end in itself is another strong point of the collection. Mr. Khalsa has been careful to adapt the exercises to different levels of social and cognitive competence. He has also provided both verbal and nonverbal options. Written formats are also available, and the exercises could easily be modified for children.

Increasingly, in this age of managed care, there will be a need for greater availability of care with greater efficiency. *Group Exercises for Enhancing Social Skills and Self-Esteem* will prove to be a valuable resource for the mental health professional in the management of group process.

Joel Levine, EdD
Psychologist / Author
Amherst, Massachusetts
June 1996

PREFACE

I am delighted to write the "Preface" to *Group Exercises for Enhancing Social Skills and Self-Esteem* because I feel it is an important contribution and resource for people in the helping professions. SiriNam Khalsa has developed a diverse collection of group process exercises which enhance the important personal element of self-esteem. Based on his extensive experience as a special educator, counselor, and group leader, the author provides therapists and educators with clear, creative, and effective methods for helping people of all ages help themselves. Each exercise in this valuable book seeks to enhance personal growth through communication and insight in a safe and nonthreatening manner.

Working with groups of differently abled people in a therapeutic and educational modality can be a powerful agent for change, and SiriNam has provided us with an easy-to-follow and effective resource for the beginning as well as experienced group leader.

Helping people to become successful in the art of living as well as prepared for dealing with life's pressures is an admirable and much-needed job. Enhancing self-esteem as well as supporting social skills awareness is the foundation for all self-growth and therapeutic work. I am aware of most of the published material available for enhancing self-esteem and social skills awareness, and I believe this book is a must for any professional who works with groups in any kind of setting.

Jack Canfield
President of the Foundation for Self-Esteem
Culver City, California
Seminar Leader, Bestselling Author of
Chicken Soup for the Soul *and*
Self-Esteem in the Classroom
June 1996

INTRODUCTION

Group Exercises for Enhancing Social Skills and Self-Esteem is a collection of activities and therapeutic exercises to assist psychotherapists, occupational and recreational therapists, teachers, and other group leaders to be more creative and effective in their group work. These exercises are designed to help a wide range of individuals including those who display depression, hyperactivity or attention deficit disorder (ADD or ADHD), personality or adjustment disorders, developmental disabilities, and general social skills deficits to become aware of acceptable social behaviors and develop proficiencies in improving their social skills.

These exercises encourage the development of the types of prosocial skills that ultimately enhance feelings of well-being and positive self-esteem. These exercises are equally applicable for use in both inpatient and outpatient settings including mental health facilities, residential and day treatment programs, schools, vocational and life skill training programs, rehabilitation and chronic care facilities, and so on.

ABOUT THIS BOOK

All of the exercises in this book are designed to stimulate group members to think creatively, expand their minds, explore their values and beliefs, and safely consider change where change is needed for personal growth. The skills that group members can acquire through these exercises should serve them well in their real day-to-day social environment. These basic social skills are the foundation building blocks for healthy human interactions in all settings. The acquisition of these skills can also be very empowering and beneficial to the self-esteem of all group participants.

The exercises in this book will help group leaders accomplish several important tasks with the group participants:

1. Guide participants in *acquiring an awareness* of what is acceptable social behavior. Each exercise includes a discussion of the importance of the concepts presented and these active discussions will aid in helping participants increase their knowledge and understanding of appropriate behaviors in a prosocial fashion.
2. Provide participants with opportunities for hands-on *practice* of new social skills in a nonthreatening environment.

Based on many years experience leading social skills training groups, I have found that in order for individuals to actually consider changing their behaviors, they need both the *awareness* of appropriate social behaviors and opportunities to *practice* new behavioral alternatives. Only when both elements are present will they learn to *use* their new skills in a personally satisfying and socially appropriate manner. Intellectual understanding of appropriate behaviors is not sufficient; individuals must also practice performing the new behaviors until they find a behavioral style that is comfortable and rewarding (both personally and socially).

Therefore, one of the tasks for the group leader is the active and deliberate teaching of desirable behaviors on both cognitive and behavioral levels. The leader will also find that these exercises will help group members develop a sense of group connectedness and cooperation. Less verbally expressive members of the group will also be motivated to more actively participate in the group process and will begin to feel more competent and positive as a result of their participation.

ENHANCING SELF-ESTEEM

As will be described below, a primary goal for therapists, teachers, and group leaders is to increase the self-esteem of group participants. This book presents direct, uncomplicated, and nonthreatening exercises to advance that goal.

WHAT IS SELF-ESTEEM?

Before we can identify low self-esteem, we need to understand what self-esteem is. We hear the word a lot these days, but what is it really? How is self-esteem enhanced or eroded in school, at work, in a family system, and during social interactions in the community? What is the relationship between self-esteem and antisocial behavior? What is the role of self-esteem in assisting group members to become what Abraham Maslow called the "self-actualized person" and the "fully human person"? (Maslow, 1962).

Self-esteem affects virtually every facet of our life. Self-esteem refers to how highly we value ourselves. It comes from collective thoughts, feelings, and experiences we have had and continue to have about ourselves throughout life. Self-esteem has been defined by the National Association for Self-Esteem as follows: *"Self-esteem is the experience of being capable of managing life's challenges and being worthy of happiness"* (1995). People who feel good about themselves usually express their feelings in their behavior as well as in an openness to learn and grow from life's lessons. They are more able to meet and solve the problems, stresses, and responsibilities of life with confidence.

SIGNS OF LOW SELF-ESTEEM

People can manifest low self-esteem in many ways. They may not even be aware that they do not feel good about themselves, though they know something is wrong.

A pioneer in self-esteem research, Nathaniel Branden (1969), explains it this way:

Consider that if an individual felt inadequate to face the challenges of life, if an individual lacked fundamental self-trust, confidence in his or her mind, we would recognize the presence of a self-esteem deficiency, no matter what other assets he or she possessed. Or if an individual lacked a basic sense of self-respect, or felt undeserving of love, unentitled to happiness, fearful of asserting thoughts, feelings or needs - again we would recognize a self-esteem deficiency, no matter what other positive attributes he or she exhibited. (p. 22)

Some common signs of low self-esteem are whining, needing to win, cheating in games, perfectionism, and exaggerated bragging; resorting to numerous attention-getting behaviors such as clowning, acting overly silly, teasing, complaining, and exhibiting both verbal and physical aggression; being self-critical, overpleasing, criticism avoidant, withdrawn, blaming, always apologizing, and fearful of success and new experiences; over- and underreacting, being unable to make choices or solve problems; expressing a narrow range of emotions and feelings, demeaning one's own talents, avoiding anxiety-provoking situations, and exhibiting antisocial behaviors.

Dealing directly with group members' self-esteem to promote healthy, socially accepted behaviors as opposed to using external punishers and reinforcers is analogous to curing illness by treating the cause rather than providing temporary relief by treating the symptoms. The exercises in this book can assist the group leader as well as empower group participants to directly promote self-esteem and prosocial skills. In a controlled study in three school districts (Reasoner, 1992), the use of a self-esteem program based on systematic training was found to significantly reduce the incidence of antisocial behavior in schools.

When people exhibit poor social skills and low self-esteem, the process of regaining their self-confidence to change behaviors and attitudes takes time. With consistent focus, the group leader can create opportunities for all group members to get in touch with their own potency and feel comfortable in their group environment as well as in themselves. *Group Exercises for Enhancing Social Skills and Self-Esteem* can help people give up negative self-messages and develop positive ones.

GENERAL GUIDELINES

This book provides the group leader with a series of structured exercises that promote dynamic positive group interactions and learning experiences. Most exercises are accompanied by an activity sheet which will serve as the catalyst for group discussions and interactions. Step-by-step instructions for the group are also included with each exercise. This format enables the group leader to "teach to the objective" in a way that is not only easier and more efficient in terms of effort and time, but also fulfills prevailing clinical and educational needs for accountability.

The following suggestions should be considered when using these exercises:

1. Before beginning each group session, identify your goals for that session, select appropriate exercises to further those goals, and review the instructions for those exercises. Make sure you have sufficient quantities of all required materials to conduct the exercises; the necessary materials are listed at the beginning of each exercise.

2. State the purpose of each exercise before it begins. This will focus both the leader and the group on the goals for the session and will help participants understand the benefits of active participation. If group members regard an exercise as meaningful in their lives, they are far more likely to be active participants who learn from the experience.

3. The description of each exercise acts as a basic road map that will assist the leader in "teaching to the objective." Each group discussion description provides in-depth directions on how the leader can promote verbal interaction, skill enhancement, and group cooperation.

4. The leader may periodically want to modify an exercise to insure that it more effectively addresses the needs of group members. Many of the exercises include suggestions for possible variations and adaptations.

5. In my experience, understanding and acceptance of the concept of diversity can best be accomplished by forming groups in which group members represent a wide range of abilities, interests, aptitudes, and backgrounds. Such heterogeneous grouping is preferred while simultaneously attempting to form a homogeneous group with respect to shared social skill deficits.

6. Participants learn best when they have an emotional investment in what is being taught. For that reason, many of the exercises in this book are "open ended" in a way that permits the leader to encourage participants to attach personal experiences, thoughts, and emotions to them.

A FEW WORDS ABOUT COOPERATIVE LEARNING

Dishon and Wilson O'Leary (1994) present a *cooperative learning* model that increases the effectiveness of the learning environment when teaching academic and social skills, as well as democratic values.

The therapeutic exercises presented in this book adhere to the basic principles of *cooperative learning models:*

1. *Heterogeneous Grouping.* The most effective groups are varied in terms of social background, cognitive skill levels, gender, and physical capabilities. The group is randomly formed or selected by the group leader to insure heterogeneity.
2. *Social Skills Acquisition.* Social skills or the ability to work cooperatively are learned skills that can be directly taught. As group participants practice the skill-building exercises, discuss the process, and observe the group interactions, they learn cooperative social skills.

Although group leaders can effectively use the exercises in this book without extensive training in group process or the concepts of cooperative learning, references are included for those readers who may want to learn more about the principles and implementation of cooperative group strategies.

YOUR ROLE AS GROUP LEADER

The group leader needs to:

1. Diagnose and understand the needs of group members including their social skill deficits and dimensions of their self-esteem.
2. Introduce exercises and facilitate meaningful group activities and discussion. It is essential that the leader be adequately prepared for each group session. This includes thoughtful consideration of the goals for the session, needs of group members, and how to teach to the objective, as well as preparation for leading the group in the specific exercises chosen for the session.
3. Know when to observe and when to guide the group process.
4. Facilitate discussion with both large and small groups.
5. Adapt the content and process of each session and each exercise to the specific needs of the group and the members of the group.
6. Introduce each exercise in a way that "sets the stage" for the participants and prepares them for the task that follows. It is critically important that all group members understand what they are being asked to do. If some members don't understand, the leader might encourage other group members to help increase their understanding. Such mentoring by group members increases group cohesiveness, cooperation, and the group learning process.

7. Expect to see an increased awareness among group members of their attitudes, beliefs, and feelings. The effective group leader learns to tap into this awareness to help group members increase their self-awareness, sense of self (including self-esteem), and positive behaviors.

Here are some additional thoughts and suggestions for the novice group leader:

1. Choose the setting for the group carefully. When participants are in a comfortable and relaxed environment, they will typically behave in a more relaxed fashion and will be more comfortable in expressing themselves. Consider having group members sit in a circle, because this arrangement promotes eye contact, interaction, and cohesiveness.
2. In general, restrain your urge to fill silence with questions or recounting of personal experiences. It sometimes takes time and a little silent support for group members to collect their thoughts, recall personal experiences, convey their feelings, and think about what they want to say. Be patient.
3. Encourage all group members to participate by making the group a safe and supportive place for all members to express themselves. Establish a climate within the group where all members always have the freedom to respond, or not respond, without fear of judgment, sanction, or pressure from others.
4. Trust is an essential ingredient for furthering human relationships. In order for the group to progress in pursuing the goals and reaching the objectives of these exercises, the group leader must foster the development of a climate of trust in which group members feel genuine caring and empathy.

USING THE EXPRESSIVE ARTS

The exercises in this book rely heavily upon the expressive mediums of writing, drawing, painting, sculpting, and role-playing to facilitate changes in social skills and self-concept. Although some of the exercises in this book incorporate elements of traditional symbolic teaching (e.g., 2 + 2 = 4), the emphasis in most of the exercises is on experiential learning using inexpensive mediums. Abraham Maslow identified "learning one's identity" as an essential ingredient for personal change. He stressed that psychoeducation that incorporates the expressive arts "can be a glimpse into one's ultimate values" (Maslow, 1962). In my experience, integrating the use of the expressive arts into social skills training provides nonthreatening modalities for helping group members discover their hidden abilities and increase their sense of self-worth.

The director of the New England Art Therapy Institute, Dale Schwartz, believes that using art as an expressive medium can provide people of all ages and learning styles with concrete images that help them reflect and find the power to change. She also stated that "the use of the expressive arts helps us express feelings and ideas for which we might not have words. It also gives us a safe way to express ourselves" (D. Schwartz, 1995, New England Art Therapy Institute).

When introducing these exercises, remind participants that artistic talent is not important; instead, stress that what is important is the willingness of all group members to freely express themselves. The group leader should also emphasize the noncompetitive and nonjudgmental nature of these exercises and insure compliance with that mandate. Edith Kramer emphasized that "when self-esteem is low, competition does not act as a stimulus; it leads to despair" (1971).

SELECTING EXERCISES

The listing below suggests exercises that might be most helpful for the various stages in the group process. It also includes the types and ages of participants that might benefit most from each exercise.

Exercises especially effective for groups in their early stages of development
Exercises 1, 3, 4, 5, 7, 11, 14, 25, 31, 36, 38

Exercises especially effective for groups in their later stages of development
Exercises 2, 6, 9, 12, 17, 18, 23, 27, 32, 34, 35, 37, 45, 51, 52, 55, 56.

Exercises especially effective for groups in any stage of development
Exercises 8, 10, 13, 15, 16, 19, 20, 21, 22, 24, 26, 28, 29, 30, 33, 39, 40, 41, 42, 43, 44, 46, 47, 48, 49, 50, 57, 58, 59, 60

Exercises especially effective for groups with participants displaying hyperactivity or Attention Deficit Disorders (ADD or ADHD)
Exercises 7, 11, 17, 19, 20, 21, 22, 24, 30, 39, 40, 49, 53, 54, 58, 59

Exercises especially effective for younger aged group participants
Exercises 2, 3, 7, 25, 43, 53

RESOURCES

Bean, R. (1992). *The Four Conditions of Self-Esteem,* Santa Cruz, CA: ETR Associates.

Branden, N. (1969). *Psychology of Self-Esteem.* Los Angeles: Bantam.

Daley, T. (1984). *Art as Therapy: An Introduction to the Use of Art as a Therapeutic Technique.* New York: Tavistock.

Dishon, D., & Wilson O'Leary, P. (1994). *A Guidebook for Cooperative Learning.* Holmes Beach, FL: Learning Publications.

Goldstein, A. P. (1988). *The Prepared Curriculum: Teaching Prosocial Competencies.* Champaign, IL: Research Press.

Khalsa, S., & Levine, J. (1993). *Talking on Purpose: Practical Skill Development for Effective Communication.* Oceanside, CA: Academic Communication Associates.

Kramer, E. (1971). *Children and Art Therapy.* New York: Schocken.

Maslow, A. (1962). *Toward a Psychology of Being.* New York: Van Nostrand.

The National Association for Self-Esteem. (1995). *Self-Esteem Today* (Vol. 8, No. 4). Santa Cruz, CA: Author.

Perls, F. (1971). *Gestalt Therapy Now.* New York: Harper and Row.

Reasoner, R. (1992, April). What's behind self-esteem programs: Truth or trickery? *The School Executive, 1,* 1-20.

Sharan, Y., & Shlomo, S. (1992). *Expanding Cooperative Learning Through Group Investigation.* New York: Teachers College Press, Columbia University.

Yalom, I. D. (1985). *The Theory and Practice of Group Psychotherapy.* New York: Basic Books.

Group Exercises
For Enhancing
Social Skills and
Self-Esteem

Connecting Circle

Purpose:

1. To facilitate group cohesiveness and relationship building.
2. To develop active listening skills.
3. To increase memory skills.

Materials:

None.

Description:

A. The group members are asked to sit in a large circle. The group leader explains that one way to help remember someone's name is by associating it with something about them. An example is given: "My name is Phyllis Vita and I love to cook Italian food."
B. The leader then introduces himself or herself and states a personal hobby or special interest in the preceding format. The participants are asked to take turns doing the same and then repeat the name and hobby of the group member who preceded them.
C. This is continued until all group members have introduced themselves and stated a special interest.

Group Discussion:

- If a group participant cannot remember all the names and/or special interests of the preceding group members, he or she should be encouraged to ask each participant their name and special interest.
- This exercise can be a lot of fun but can also create some anxiety among participants with a short attention span or poor memory skills. The group leader should be aware of participants' disabilities and create a supportive atmosphere by explaining the option of asking each member their name and special interest.
- This exercise is especially effective as an icebreaker for the beginning of a group session.

Box Full of Me

Purpose:

1. To increase a person's understanding of how significant events influenced or affected his or her own life.
2. To gain acceptance of each other's positive and negative personal past events.
3. To reinforce group communication skills.

Materials:

Cardboard box; paper; writing materials.

Description:

A. A box with the words "Box Full of Me" written on it is placed in the center of the group circle. The leader has previously placed a paper in the box.
B. Members listen while the leader opens the box and reads a paragraph on a piece of paper that describes a significant event that occurred in the leader's life in the past 5 years. Leader explains how this event has affected his or her life in the present.
C. Members are asked to write three sentences or a paragraph describing a significant past event (either negative or positive).
D. The group leader places folded papers with members' names written on them in the "Box Full of Me."
E. As the leader randomly pulls out a paper, the name is read out loud and given to each group member who takes a turn reading his or her personal past events to the whole group.
F. *Variations:*
   ✓ Group members can write sentences or paragraphs of significant events that took place in the past year, week, or day.
   ✓ The leader can ask members to bring in a photo of themselves, write a paragraph on what they were thinking or doing at that time, and then share with the group.

Group Discussion:

- Members tell how past events might have affected their lives in the present. *For example:* John wrote that he remembers watching his grandfather planting tomatoes in his garden and how enjoyable it was to watch vegetables grow, then pick them and prepare a delicious meal. It affected John's present life because even though his grandfather has passed away, John now makes an effort to plant his own tomatoes and is proud of his summer vegetable garden.
- The group leader will often need to interpret or facilitate the understanding of how each event has affected members' lives.
- This exercise can be used with a variety of groups who have already established some interpersonal skills.

Circle of Hands

Purpose:

1. To experience the importance of connecting relationships within the group.
2. To encourage group identity regardless of race, religion, gender, disability, and so on.

Materials:

Colored construction paper; scissors; markers; tape.

Description:

A. The leader asks the group to think about a part of their body that has the ability to show kind affection and also angry aggression. It can be used for connecting relationships but also for pushing people away (hands).
B. Each participant is asked to sit with a partner and to take turns outlining each other's hands on a piece of construction paper. Cut out hands and initial each one.
C. The leader tapes hands on the wall or bulletin board, interconnecting them in a large circle. Members write their name on each of their hands.

Group Discussion:

- The group discusses the symbolism of a large interconnecting circle of hands and the feelings evoked by the image.
- Members are also encouraged to discuss ways in which hands are used to communicate inner thoughts and feelings.
- This exercise is a good one to use at the beginning of a group's formation, because it builds a sense of group connectedness in a nonthreatening way.

Can't Judge a Box By Its Cover

Purpose:

1. To promote appreciation of individual differences.
2. To encourage participants to look beyond physical appearance when establishing relationships.
3. To explore various ways of getting to know one another.

Materials:

One shoe box; paper bag; dollar bill; wrapping paper; undesirable object (such as old lemon, potato, or onion). One copy of the "Knowing Someone" activity sheet for each member.

Description:

A. The group leader prepares the shoe box by wrapping it as a present so the lid comes off. The leader then places the undesirable object in the box. In the crumpled paper bag should be placed the dollar bill.
B. Leader places the box and bag in the center of the group circle and asks members of the group which object they would choose, not knowing the contents.
C. Two members are chosen to first open the box and show its contents, and then do the same with the bag.
D. Members are paired up and asked to fill out their activity sheet "Knowing Someone."

Group Discussion:

- After the contents of the box and bag have been revealed, group members are encouraged to discuss the significance of what just occurred.
- Members are asked to define the meaning of "You can't judge a book by its cover."
- During the discussion, the leader should take an active role in helping members explore alternative ways of getting to know someone. Using the metaphor of the box, emphasize the importance of getting to know someone by looking beyond his or her physical appearance.
- Members are then paired and asked to fill out their activity sheets. They then can share their work with the group.
- This exercise has worked well with a wide variety of age groups and abilities.

Knowing Someone

Directions: It often takes time to get to know more about someone than you might guess by the way he or she looks, talks, or acts. In this exercise, write on each line a personal statement about your partner (e.g., personal likes and dislikes, hobbies, etc.).

Being Part of the Group

Purpose:

1. To encourage group cohesion by identifying with a mutual problem.
2. To promote interaction by sharing viewpoints.
3. To increase attitudes of group inclusion.

Materials:

One copy of the "Marion and the Group" activity sheet for each member; writing materials.

Description:

A. The leader initiates a discussion about feelings having to do with being left out of a group. Members are encouraged to share their experiences.
B. The group leader reads aloud the story "Marion and the Group" and asks members to listen closely. Each member is given an activity sheet to fill out independently.
C. When the activity sheets are completed, all group members sit in a circle and discuss their answers. Afterwards, volunteers are asked to role-play their answers for the group.

Group Discussion:

- The group's discussion first centers on the answers given by members. The leader helps to identify responses that are similar and those that are different. Members are then encouraged to express a personal value that corresponds to their viewpoint (e.g., "I think helping someone feel comfortable when they are in a new situation takes courage").
- Members are asked to discuss their answers to question #4, and whether or not they would do things differently after completing the activity sheet.
- When the members are asked to role-play their answers, individuals should experience a role not normally their own. The leader then encourages discussion about their feelings and any change in attitudes toward solving the problem of inclusion in a group.
- This exercise is effective with groups in the initial stages of development.

Marion and the Group

Directions: Read the following story, then answer the questions below. A large group of students at Smith High School get together at lunch to talk about activities for the weekend. They talk about activities such as going to the movies, playing sports, and socializing at each other's houses.

Marion recently transferred to Smith High School. He was new and didn't make friends easily. Marion wanted to be part of this group of students so he could socialize with people his own age on the weekends. Nobody in the group ever made an effort to speak to him, and he never talked to any of them. He didn't know what to say or do.

1. What could Marion do to become part of the group?

_____

_____

_____

_____

2. Should the people in the group invite Marion to join them? Why?

_____

_____

_____

_____

3. Think of some things that Marion could say to start a conversation with members of the group.

_____

_____

_____

_____

4. Have you ever been in a situation where you found it difficult to meet new people? How did it make you feel? What did you do?

_____

_____

_____

_____

Giving and Receiving Positive Statements

Purpose:

1. To enhance self-esteem by encouraging recognition of positive attributes in each other.
2. To increase group connectedness.
3. To define positive qualities in a descriptive manner.

Materials:

Large sheets of newsprint; magic markers; instant camera such as a Polaroid; small pieces of paper; shoe box or other medium-sized container; writing materials.

Description:

A. Group members write their name on a small piece of paper and place it folded into a container. The group leader tapes a large piece of newsprint on the wall with the words "Person of the Week" written on the top. The leader explains that everyone has many positive qualities. For example, "Dee, you have a great sense of humor," or "Jamel, you're a great dresser."

B. A participant is chosen to draw one name from the container which is given to the group leader. The leader expresses a few descriptive positive qualities about the person chosen without reading his or her name. For example, "This person loves sports and has a great smile."

C. The leader then announces the person's name and shakes his or her hand to congratulate the person on being picked as "Person of the Week." A photograph is then taken of the chosen group member and taped underneath "Person of the Week."

D. Five to 10 group members are asked to state the qualities they like about the chosen group member. The leader writes these qualities under the person's photo. After all positive qualities have been written on the paper, each member is asked again to state what they like about the person of the week by looking at him or her and stating it directly. For example, someone might say, "Lisa, I really like the way you laugh," and then Lisa would acknowledge the compliment by saying "Thank you."

E. *Variation:* Each participant writes their positive statement underneath the photo.

Group Discussion:

- The leader asks the members to describe why it is important to acknowledge positive attributes or qualities in each other. The leader helps the group reflect on its own dynamics of giving and receiving positive statements.
- Each member is reminded that it could be his or her turn in the future and should be encouraged, though not required, to participate by expressing something.
- This exercise is most effective with groups that are beyond the early stage of development.

Acceptable Touching

Purpose:

1. To identify incidents concerning the appropriate touching of others.
2. To increase awareness of when appropriate touching is acceptable.

Materials:

"Acceptable Touching" activity sheet for each member; writing materials; yardstick.

Description:

A. The group leader introduces this lesson by explaining that some people enjoy touching or physical contact with others; others prefer not to be touched. The leader asks if anyone in the group has ever been upset because of unacceptable touching by others such as tapping, pushing, shoving, and so on.

B. The group members are asked to stand facing each other at a comfortable distance apart. The leader uses the yardstick to measure this distance and explains that this distance can be called one's "comfort zone." Members are asked to slowly walk closer to each other until they feel uncomfortable. Measure the distance between them and compare this with the comfort zone distance.

 Two other group members are asked to repeat the same exercise and compare "comfort zone" distances.

C. Members are asked to fill out the "Acceptable Touching" activity sheets. The leader facilitates a follow-up discussion with the group.

Group Discussion:

- The participants discuss responses to the items. Topics for discussion can include: Under what circumstances could some aggressive physical contact be acceptable? (*Examples:* sports, competition with friends.) Or, discuss why someone who doesn't like to be physically close to others may not appreciate even light touching, while another person might enjoy a pat on the back.
- The leader should stress that people are different and it is important that members become sensitive about what is acceptable and not acceptable touch with another person before they get too aggressive with him or her.
- This exercise works well with groups in the initial stages of development.

Acceptable Touching

Directions: Is this touching acceptable or not acceptable? Write **yes** or **no** on each line.

1. Shaking someone's hand.   _____

2. Giving a friend the "high five" slap.   _____

3. Touching someone's backside.   _____

4. Pushing someone in the back.   _____

5. Poking someone in the arm to get their attention.   _____

6. Slapping someone on the arm.   _____

7. Rubbing someone's shoulders.   _____

8. Bumping into someone with your shoulder.   _____

9. Putting your arm around someone's shoulder.   _____

10. Giving someone a "bear hug."   _____

My Role Models

Purpose:

1. To gain a greater understanding of positive role models and their influence on people's lives.
2. To identify and write about positive role models in one's life.

Materials:

Paper; writing materials; blackboard or newsprint pad.

Description:

A. The leader writes the words "Role Model" on the board and asks participants to define each word. (*Models:* reference points that provide us with human, philosophical, and operational examples that help in establishing meaningful values, goals, and personal standards in life.)
B. The group leader talks about someone he or she admires or admired when young (mother, father, teacher, athlete, etc.) and how that person affected his or her life then and now. An explanation of the importance of models in our lives is given.
C. Group members are asked to choose one or two people they believe are positive role models. Then each member is given a piece of paper and pen and asked to write a one-page essay focusing on the qualities that make their role model special.
D. Encourage group members to share their essays with others either in small groups or by volunteering to read them out loud in the large group.

Group Discussion:

- Before and after the essays are written, group members are encouraged to discuss and share their ideas of what makes a positive role model and why.
- If some members have difficulty identifying a role model in their life, the leader should offer suggestions such as well-known athletes, politicians, actors, musicians, and so on.
- This exercise may be used with a variety of groups in any stage of development.

What I Value

Purpose:

1. To recognize personal values.
2. To increase understanding of other group members' values.
3. To further develop a healthy belief system that can guide one through life's decisions.

Materials:

One copy of the "What I Value" activity sheet for each member; writing materials.

Description:

A. The group leader asks for a definition of a value and then gives a complete definition.
B. Ask group members to name some common values and how values might develop (from family members, peers, TV, reading, religion, etc.).
C. Each member is then given an activity sheet and asked to spend 5 to 10 minutes answering the questions. If necessary, questions can be read aloud by the leader or each participant.
D. When the activity sheet is completed, the group is divided into small groups. Each group is asked to discuss their responses to the questions.

Group Discussion:

- The following can be used as a definition of a value: "A value is a belief or a feeling that something is worthwhile. It could be an idea, a course of action, or something you do. A true value can be talked about, is based on personal choice, and comes up regularly in one's life. You count on values to guide your decisions in life."
- After giving this definition, ask for examples of values and discuss whether they are true values based on this definition.
- The leader guides each group's discussion by encouraging members to identify similarities and differences of expressed personal values, emphasizing the need to *not judge* answers as right or wrong.
- This exercise is most effective in groups that have developed a certain degree of mutual trust and openness with each other.

What I Value

Directions: Please read each statement and then check the most likely answer(s).

1. My house is on fire. Everyone else has escaped. If I had time to take one thing out of the house, I would take

   ____ my pet
   ____ my favorite article of clothing
   ____ my stereo (or radio or TV)
   ____ my diary
   ____ my money
   ____ other _____

2. If my friends want me to try an illegal drug, I would

   ____ do so
   ____ refuse and try to talk them out of it
   ____ refuse and later tell their parents about their drug-taking
   ____ refuse but stay with them and say nothing
   ____ refuse and walk away from them
   ____ other _____

3. If my best friend started smoking cigarettes, I would

   ____ join in
   ____ say nothing
   ____ try to talk my friend out of it
   ____ tell my friend's parents
   ____ collect information about the dangers of cigarettes and show it to my friend
   ____ other _____

4. If my father started drinking heavily, I would

   ____ beg him to stop
   ____ say nothing and stay out of his way
   ____ contact our family doctor or minister
   ____ stay away from home as much as possible
   ____ hide his alcohol
   ____ other _____

5. If my friend asked me to participate in shoplifting, I would

   ____ refuse and end our friendship
   ____ go along
   ____ try to talk my friend out of it
   ____ tell my friend's parents
   ____ refuse but continue our relationship
   ____ other _____

6. If I could make all the decisions about my education, I would

   ____ quit school right away
   ____ go to college and earn a degree
   ____ go to a vocational school and learn a trade
   ____ stay right where I am
   ____ other _____

7. If I were rich, I would spend my money on

   ____ education
   ____ travel
   ____ possessions
   ____ my friends
   ____ my family
   ____ other _____

8. I feel happiest when

   ____ I make my parents proud of me
   ____ I am liked and accepted by my friends
   ____ I do well in school
   ____ I feel I know myself
   ____ something I've planned works out
   ____ other _____

9. I feel most sad when

   ____ I disappoint a friend
   ____ I disappoint my parents
   ____ I don't do as well as I should in school
   ____ someone doesn't like me
   ____ I feel confused, and don't know who I am
   ____ other _____

10. If I could change one thing in the world, I would

    ____ stop all wars
    ____ end poverty
    ____ make myself a better person
    ____ make an unhappy friend happy
    ____ make an unhappy family member happy
    ____ other _____

What Are My Values?

Purpose:

    1. To recognize personal values.

    2. To increase understanding of how personal values affect lifestyle decisions.

    3. To explore similarities and differences among group members' personal values.

Materials:

    One copy of the "What Are My Values?" activity sheet for each member; writing materials.

Description:

    A. The group leader asks each member to fill out the activity sheet. If necessary, questions can be read aloud by the leader.

    B. When the activity sheet is completed, the group is divided into four teams; A, B, C, and D.

    C. Assign each team the corresponding category of A, B, C, or D from the activity sheet to discuss their individual responses. For example, Team A will discuss what's very important or not so important about where they live. Team D will share their thoughts about how they spend their free time.

    D. Leader will pick a spokesperson from each team to summarize each team's discussion to the large group.

    E. *Variation:* Each team is asked to cut out pictures from magazines that symbolize chosen lifestyle values. These pictures can then be pasted onto a large piece of paper, creating a "values collage." This variation works well with all age groups, regardless of abilities.

Group Discussion:

- Before handing out activity sheets to group members, a brief definition is given for a value, and how values impact upon lifestyle choices is discussed. A value is a belief or a feeling about something that's important or worthwhile. An example can be someone's belief about eating or not eating meat or recycling paper and cans, and how these values might be an important belief in their life.
- The leader encourages members to identify similarities and differences of expressed personal values and how they might affect lifestyle decisions.
- This exercise works well with many age groups at all stages of development.

What Are My Values?

A value is a belief or a feeling that something is worthwhile. It can be an idea, a course of action, a person, place, or thing. What are your values? You can test out your answers by asking yourself: Is what I value based on my own choice? Do I believe in this value so much I would be willing to tell the world about it? Is it something I cherish?

Directions: To explore your values, do the following activity. How do your values help you in choosing your lifestyle? To help you answer this question, rate the following items as (**1**) Very Important, (**2**) Somewhat Important, or (**3**) Not Important At All When You Consider. . . .

A. Where You Live

____ Safety	____ Quiet	____ Privacy
____ Type of Housing	____ Sunshine	____ Space
____ Location	____ Suburbs	____ Convenience
____ Climate	____ Environment	____ Other _____
____ Neighbors	____ Security	_____

B. Whom You Live With

____ Marriage	____ Small Family	____ Quiet House
____ Alone	____ Roommates	____ A lot of Socializing
____ Large Family	____ Pets	____ Just Boys or Girls

C. Summer Work/Career

____ Social Acceptance	____ Title	____ Status
____ Self-Esteem	____ Uniform	____ Independence
____ Personal Growth	____ Part-Time	____ Creativity
____ Self-Expression	____ Full-Time	____ Work Out-of-Doors
____ Satisfy Own Curiosity	____ Service to Others	____ Physical Work
____ Regular Hours	____ Amount of Income	____ Travel
____ Flexible Hours	____ Challenging Work	____ Other _____
____ Location	____ Glamour	_____

D. Your Free Time

____ Spend It With Others	____ Spend It Alone	____ TV
____ Sports	____ Arts and Crafts	____ Being Outdoors
____ Reading/Writing	____ Need Lots of Free Time	____ Being Indoors
____ Don't Need Very	____ Music	____ Other _____
Much Free Time	____ Movies/Videos	_____

Judging Values of Others

Purpose:

1. To increase influence of positive role models.
2. To gain a deeper understanding of others' beliefs and values.
3. To explore personal values.

Materials:

"Judging Values" activity sheet for each member; writing materials; autobiographies of choice.

Description:

A. The leader introduces the exercise by asking members if they have ever stopped to think about why people act in certain ways and how this might be influenced by their values. Comments from the group are encouraged.

B. The members are given the assignment to read about a person who interests them or whom they look up to as a role model.

C. At the next session, the leader passes out the "Judging Values" activity sheets and asks members to think about the person they read about before answering the questions.

D. Members are asked to pair up and take turns discussing their answers. The leader connects with each group to facilitate discussion.

E. Each member is asked to share one answer with the entire group.

F. *Variations:*

   ✓ I have successfully used the videotape *Michael Jordan: Come Fly With Me* to illustrate clear values and beliefs held by a popular role model. (*Michael Jordan: Come Fly With Me* can be purchased in most video stores or ordered directly from CBS/FOX Video Sports, 1211 Avenue of the Americas, New York, NY 10036.)

   ✓ Members view video, then fill out activity sheet based on the values of Michael Jordan.

Group Discussion:

- Each pair discusses the similarities and differences between their chosen role models. The leader encourages members to compare their personal beliefs and values to the person they read about.
- When the members share one answer with the whole group, the leader helps members to recognize any similarities with each others' answers.
- This exercise helps members explore different role models and belief systems.
- This exercise should be presented in the early stages of group development, especially when behavioral issues are being addressed.

Judging Values

_____

(Person's Name)

Directions: Choose any autobiography from your personal library or from the school's or public library. Then answer the following questions.

1. How would you describe this person?

   _____

   _____

   _____

2. What are this person's values?

   _____

   _____

   _____

3. What is this person for? Against?

   _____

   _____

   _____

4. Have you ever done anything like this person?

   _____

   _____

   _____

5. How did this person get to where he or she is now? What was his or her educational background? What did this person do with his or her free time?

   _____

   _____

   _____

6. Do you admire this person? Why or why not?

   _____

   _____

   _____

Right or Wrong

Purpose:

1. To help clarify values which will lend personal guidance in life decisions.
2. To promote insight and understanding of others' values.
3. To encourage cooperative skills.

Materials:

Newsprint or blackboard; magic markers.

Description:

A. The group leader asks the members to think about these questions: Have you ever been confused about what might be the right or wrong thing to do or say? For instance, you overhear a friend say something mean about another friend. What should you do? You catch your sibling lying to your parents. Do you tell them? These are not easy questions to answer.
B. Participants are asked to sit in groups of three. On the board, the leader writes words such as lying, tattling, stealing, and hitting.
C. The groups of three are asked to discuss when it might be right or wrong to do what the words describe.
D. After a 10- to 15-minute discussion, members sit in a large group and volunteers from each triad share their thoughts on "right and wrong" for the various words discussed in small groups.

Group Discussion:

- As members share their thoughts, the leader encourages others to refrain from judging whether the answers are "right or wrong." Members look for similarities and differences in personal perspectives as the discussion progresses.
- This exercise may lead to a wide variety of beliefs on what is right or wrong, and the discussion may be continued at other sessions.
- This exercise was designed for groups who have established some degree of group rapport and which are in the later stages of group development.

Pros and Cons

Purpose:

1. To explore personal beliefs and values.
2. To increase group cohesiveness and empathy.
3. To express a stand on a controversial issue and increase thought flexibility.

Materials:

Index cards; writing materials; "Topics for Discussion" activity sheet.

Description:

A. The group leader defines "pro" and "con" as arguments "for" or "against" an opinion. The group is then divided into two groups, one being the "Pro" group and the other the "Con" group. The leader then explains that each group will be given an index card showing a controversial topic to be discussed. The "Pro" group will give opinions in support of the topic, and the "Con" group will give opinions against the topic.

B. An index card with the chosen topic written on it is given to each group. After a brief discussion among group members, each member is given a chance to give a "pro" or "con" opinion, depending on which group they are in. Both groups come together (facing each other) and express their opinions.

C. After each participant makes a contribution, another index card is given to each group and the process is repeated.

D. *Variation:* The participants can make up their own topics to discuss. The group leader can switch the "Pro" and "Con" groups after a few topics have been discussed. This really challenges participants to be flexible thinkers!

Group Discussion:

- Before the first index cards are handed out, the group leader talks about what makes a topic controversial.
- After each topic is addressed, it is worthwhile to discuss the concept of having an open mind or to be able to have flexibility in thinking. Group members might benefit from sharing their feelings about speaking for or against something because of the group they were in. Questions can be asked such as, "Has this increased your understanding of how different people feel about these topics?" or "Do you feel as much pro or con about the topic after each discussion? Why or why not?"

Pros and Cons
Topics for Discussion

Directions: The group leader should write one topic on each index card. These cards will be used in accordance with the instructions for this exercise.

1. Athletic scholarships

2. AIDS testing before marriage

3. Aerobic exercise

4. Birth control

5. Boxing as a sport

6. Cosmetic surgery

7. Curfews

8. Drinking and driving

9. Drug testing in the work environment

10. Fast-food restaurants

11. Gambling

12. MTV

13. Mercy killing

14. Premarital sex

15. Professional wrestling

16. Sex education in the schools

17. Smoking in public places

18. Video games

19. Vegetarian diets

20. Working mothers

My Favorite Things

Purpose:

1. To increase awareness of personal uniqueness with enjoyable experiences in one's life.
2. To promote group cohesion by identifying similar interests.

Materials:

Art board; scissors; glue; markers; variety of magazines; chalkboard or newsprint; tape.

Description:

A. The group leader writes on a chalkboard or piece of newsprint: "These Are My Favorite: foods, sports, places, animals, people, colors, music, clothes . . . (and so on)." The leader then draws a large circle and divides it up into sections representing each "favorite thing" by labeling each section.
B. Participants are asked to sit and work in small groups of four or five members. Each group will have magazines, scissors, glue, art board, and markers. Instruct participants to draw their own circles and choose categories of "favorite things," labeling them into sections in the circle.
C. The members are asked to cut out and glue pictures from magazines, or draw their own, representing their favorite things in sections of the circle.
D. The completed collages are then displayed for discussion and appreciation.

Group Discussion:

- Members discuss their collages and explain why the things they have chosen are their favorites. They are asked if they would like to experience their "favorite things" more often.
- The group discusses what differences and similarities exist among different group members. The leader encourages members to be aware of similarities and supportive of differences by refraining from negative comments (e.g., I hate beets; they taste gross!).
- This exercise works well in early stages of group development to help members get acquainted with each other in a nonthreatening way.

"Do As I Say, Not As I Do"

Purpose:

1. To identify consistent and inconsistent behaviors in others and self.
2. To increase observation skills.
3. To promote insight into positive models.

Materials:

One copy of "Do As I Say, Not As I Do" activity sheet for each member; blackboard or newsprint; writing materials.

Description:

A. The group leader writes *"Do As I Say, Not As I Do"* on the board, and asks participants to give their thoughts on its meaning. Members are encouraged to give specific examples of its meaning, such as a parent shouting at the children to keep the "noise" down, or a cigarette smoker advising a nonsmoker to never start smoking.
B. Members are given a copy of the activity sheet and asked to fill it out individually or with a partner.
C. When finished, participants sit in a circle and two volunteers are asked to role-play an example for the group. The leader initiates a discussion of the possible negative consequences of inconsistent role modeling.

Group Discussion:

- A separate discussion should follow each role-play. The leader asks role-playing members if the "Observed Behavior or Attitude" was of someone else or of themselves.
- It might be difficult for some group members to think of examples of inconsistent behaviors to achieve desired outcomes. An option is for the leader to give them the "Desired Outcome" on the activity sheet and the participant can write a supportive and unsupportive observed behavior or attitude for positive role modeling.
- This exercise can be used with a variety of groups at all stages of development and age levels.

"Do As I Say, Not As I Do"

Directions: Fill in the three categories below, thinking about situations that have occurred in your life. If you prefer, fill this out with a partner.

Desired Outcome	Observed Behavior or Attitude	How Should the Person Have Behaved?
Example: Ask politely when wanting something.	**Person Said:** Give me some of that ice cream!	**Could Have Said:** Can I have some ice cream please?

I Want To Be Like . . .

Purpose:

1. To identify positive qualities of chosen role models.
2. To define positive qualities.
3. To develop group cohesion through self-disclosure.

Materials:

Sports, music, and celebrity magazines; tag board; scissors; rubber cement; writing materials.

Description:

A. The group leader introduces this exercise by discussing what role models are and how we can use them in a positive way.
B. The materials are placed in the center of a large table, and members are asked to look through magazines and cut out pictures of people they see as role models.
C. After identifying role models, the participants are asked to paste the cut-out pictures on a piece of tag board, leaving space below each picture for a sentence stating the role model's positive quality.
D. The collages are displayed, and the leader facilitates a discussion on what makes a positive quality.

Group Discussion:

- The leader describes role models as people who provide examples of meaningful values, goals, ideals, and personal standards to live by. They can help one to answer such questions as, How should I act? What do I believe? Whom do I respect? Whom can I look to for help? It is explained that these role models can include parents, teachers, musicians, athletes, political leaders, and ministers.
- When defining a role model's positive quality, group members sometimes use words that are evaluative rather than descriptive (e.g., "He's a nice person," versus "He helps poor people find jobs"). The leader should encourage descriptive sentences that describe the chosen role model's positive qualities.
- If members cannot find a picture of a role model, they can write the positive qualities attributed to that person and then cut out a picture symbolizing that quality (e.g., a mountain for strength and courage, the sun for guidance, a mother animal with her baby for love and caring).
- This exercise can be successfully used with all age groups and at any stage of development.

Finding Happiness

Purpose:

1. To increase awareness of role models for personal happiness.
2. To gain an understanding of what makes people feel happy.
3. To explore how people can positively affect each other.

Materials:

One copy of "Looking at Happiness" activity sheet for each member; writing materials.

Description:

A. The group leader begins this exercise by asking members to define what happiness means to them. They discuss what makes them feel happy and why.
B. The leader states: "Happiness is a state of mind or a way we think about life. Happiness is also something we can learn from others." Members discuss how many times they have seen others enjoying themselves and feeling happy. The leader asks if anyone ever wanted to find out why others are feeling good and if being around people who feel happy can "rub off" onto them.
C. While handing out the "Looking at Happiness" activity sheets, the leader explains that one way to understand how to create happiness in one's life is to observe others who often feel happy about life.
D. Leader asks for volunteers to share their answers with the group.

Group Discussion:

- The leader helps members to explore whether this exercise was helpful by summarizing the group members' responses. The leader reminds the participants that by observing other people's happiness, they can learn the habits and behaviors these people have in common which promote happiness in their lives.
- After members answer #5 on the activity sheet, they might find it helpful to discuss the positive influences role models can possibly have on their own behavior and thinking.
- This exercise is effective with groups that may need help with behavior guidelines and decision-making skills.

Looking at Happiness

Directions: Please read each question and give yourself a few minutes to think about your response before writing it down.

1. Think about your parents or guardians. How do you know when they are feeling happy?

_____

_____

_____

_____

2. What are some specific things that (you think) make them happy?

_____

_____

_____

_____

3. How do you feel when they are feeling good? Why?

_____

_____

_____

_____

4. Think about other people in your life: friends, siblings, or relatives. How do you know when they are happy?

_____

_____

_____

_____

5. List ways these people have positively affected the way you think and act.

_____

_____

_____

_____

_____

Who's in Control?

Purpose:

1. To increase awareness of personal beliefs and values concerning parental input and control.
2. To increase understanding of how personal beliefs might influence the circumstances of group members' lives.

Materials:

One copy of the "Who's in Control?" activity sheet for each member; chalkboard or newsprint; writing materials.

Description:

A. The group leader begins this exercise by saying, "Parents are often trying to decide how much control or influence they should have over their children's lives regardless of their ages. When children become teenagers, their inner desire becomes *to not need their parents*. A parent's inner desire usually continues to be *I need to be needed by my child*. What do you think of this conflict of needs?" A short discussion should take place.
B. On a board or newsprint the leader then writes (a) "What are the advantages and disadvantages of parental influence?" (b) "How much responsibility should parents have for influencing their children's actions and decisions?" The group leader then facilitates another short discussion.
C. "Who's in Control?" activity sheets are handed out and each participant is asked to carefully think about each question before answering.
D. *Variations:* Ask group members to form groups of four and role-play these scenarios:

  ✓ One person is feeling really down because he or she wants to try out for a sports team. The person's parents have not supported this because they are concerned that their son or daughter will get injured. Have one group member play a parent, another the coach of the team, and a third the son or daughter. The fourth member should observe the role-play and offer his or her impression of what dynamic is occurring between the family members.
  ✓ Four people are discussing their summer plans. One person will be working as a lifeguard, another will be going to a summer camp, a third will be going away to ballet school, and the last one says he or she will "hang out" at home.

Group Discussion:

- While discussing answers in a group, focus on personal beliefs and values concerning parental input and influence. Remind participants that every situation is different and that their answers are not right or wrong but should be discussed without judgment.
- This exercise works best with an established group that is capable of insight.
- *Questions for Discussion Include:*

  ▷ Why do you think they are choosing these activities?
  ▷ What do these activities say about each person's lifestyle?

Who's in Control?

Directions: Look at the cartoon below and then answer the following questions.

"In 10 more minutes you can stop practicing the piano!"

1. Do you think parents should force their children into activities they don't really like? Is it for their own good?

   _____

   _____

   _____

2. Should parents play a part in their child's lifestyle now or in the future?

   _____

   _____

   _____

3. Who controls your lifestyle?

   _____

   _____

   _____

4. What will be your philosophy for your own children should you decide to have them?

   _____

   _____

   _____

Looking at Stress

Purpose:

1. To define stress and identify sources of stress in one's life.
2. To explore similarities and differences in the experiences of life's stressors.

Materials:

One copy of "My Stress" activity sheet for each member; writing materials.

Description:

A. The group leader will begin by discussing the relationship between self and stress by saying, "Stress is created in the body and mind, especially when people are feeling tired, worried, or pressured. Consequently, conflicts are more likely to occur when stressed than when feeling rested, confident, and in control."
B. The leader distributes the "My Stress" self-assessment activity sheets to each participant, reviews the directions, and gives the participants 5 to 10 minutes to write down their responses.
C. Have the members form groups of three to discuss their self-assessments. Suggest that they compare items to discover similarities and differences, and then select one item on the activity sheet for which they all circled the number 5.
D. The leader asks each group to discuss what makes the chosen item so stressful.

For Example:

I am concerned about dying.   1   ③   5

"My grandmother just died and I really miss her. It also makes me wonder where she went."

Group Discussion:

- It's important during the beginning discussion for the leader to point out that when people are experiencing stress, they need to identify what is bothering them so they can eliminate the problem and/or effectively cope with the stress.
- The leader should also emphasize, however, that not all stressors can be eliminated. Some cannot even be reduced. For example, if one's parents are getting divorced, one has little or no control over the situation.
- This exercise should precede the "Reducing Stress" exercise (Exercise 20).
- Groups that are in all stages of development can benefit from this exercise.

My Stress

Directions: Please read this list of possible stressors and then rate yourself on each statement with a 1, 3, or 5. Circle **1** on the scale if you **never** experience this kind of stress. Circle **3** if you **sometimes** experience this kind of stress and circle **5** if you **frequently** experience this kind of stress.

1. I am concerned about dying.   1   3   5

2. I am concerned about my health.   1   3   5

3. I am concerned about violence.   1   3   5

4. I am concerned about not being loved.   1   3   5

5. I am concerned about my weight.   1   3   5

6. I am concerned about being shy.   1   3   5

7. I am concerned about my work.   1   3   5

8. I am concerned about making friends.   1   3   5

9. I am concerned about not fitting in at school.   1   3   5

10. I am concerned about responsibilities I have.   1   3   5

11. I am concerned about money.   1   3   5

12. I am concerned about the environment.   1   3   5

13. I am concerned about my family.   1   3   5

14. I am concerned about _____ .   1   3   5

Reducing Stress

Purpose:

1. To explore reasons for reducing stress.
2. To describe effective methods of reducing stress.

Materials:

Paper; writing materials; blackboard or newsprint.

Description:

A. Group leader asks for a definition of stress and identifies sources of stress in group members' lives.

B. The group members are then asked to make a list of (or brainstorm) effective methods of reducing stress. List their ideas on the board. Include such items as:

- Sleep
- Listen to music
- Go for a jog or walk
- Play a musical instrument
- Scream into a pillow
- Breathe deeply, meditate, or do yoga
- Talk with a friend
- Play a sport, do aerobic exercise, or dance

C. Participants are then asked to make a list of the methods they would most likely use.

Group Discussion:

- When each member identifies the methods of reducing stress they would use, they should be encouraged to discuss whether they are using these methods, and if not, why?
- Members also should explore the possible consequences to the body and mind of not releasing stress. These consequences can include emotions of anger or frustration, muscular tension, headaches, insomnia, and so on.
- This exercise can be successfully used at all stages of the group's development. The leader might want to introduce the stress-reducing exercises in the early stages of a group whose members are exhibiting hyperactive behavior and/or short attention span.

Ways to Manage My Stress

Purpose:

1. To help plan strategies for handling stressful situations.
2. To increase group support for stress-releasing habits.

Materials:

"Managing My Stress" activity sheet for each member; writing materials.

Description:

A. The group leader introduces this exercise by explaining how we all need to take responsibility for our emotional health from time to time; otherwise, we can become physically ill or mentally unbalanced.
B. The group members are asked to give a few examples of strategies they presently might use for handling stressful situations (e.g., getting enough sleep, eating nutritious foods).
C. The "Ways to Manage Stress" activity sheets are handed out to each group participant. The leader asks members to try to be completely honest when rating themselves on each statement. If reading ability and comprehension level of participants are low, statements can be read aloud by the group leader, then answered by each participant.
D. Group members are asked to score themselves when completed with activity sheets. Pair up for discussion.

Group Discussion:

- The group leader explains that if the participants score between 10 and 25, then there are several areas they need to develop to better release their stress level. They can discuss some of their answers with their partners.
- If they scored between 25 and 37, the participants have discovered a variety of ways to deal effectively with stress. They should discuss those items that were checked "Need to improve" and find ways to move them to "I'm average."
- If group participants scored 37 or greater, they should be congratulated for finding excellent ways to deal with life's stresses. They should be reminded to discuss ways to keep themselves alert to continuing these valuable behaviors they have acquired.
- This exercise is effective with many group types at all stages of development.

Managing My Stress

Directions: Please rate yourself on each question with a **5** for "I do well"; a **3** for "I'm average"; or a **1** for "Need to improve."

I am succeeding at:

_____ 1. Scheduling time for enjoyable activities.

_____ 2. Getting enough sleep at night.

_____ 3. Not taking on more than I can handle (learning to say no).

_____ 4. Having a physical fitness program that involves strenuous exercise.

_____ 5. Practicing relaxation.

_____ 6. Eating nutritious foods and avoiding junk foods.

_____ 7. Avoiding alcohol or drugs.

_____ 8. Planning regular recreation that's fun.

_____ 9. Talking out troubles and getting professional help if needed.

_____ 10. Having a good laugh at least once per day.

Now score yourself by totaling your numbers.

Stress Away

Purpose:

    1. To increase body awareness and the ability to control inner stress and its effect on outer behavior.
    2. To promote active listening skills and group cohesiveness.

Materials:

    Tape player; Stress Control Cards* (SCC); "Progressive Relaxation Sequence" activity sheet; poster paper; colored markers.

Description:

    A. Group leader begins this exercise by asking participants to define what being "stressed out" means.
    B. It is then explained to members how stress affects the body, and how stress is measured using the stress control cards (see "Group Discussion").
    C. Participants are asked to sit in a circle and an SCC is placed on the floor in front of their chairs until they are instructed to pick it up. With card in hand, participants are then instructed to press lightly with their thumb on the black square for 10 seconds.
    D. The leader counts silently to 10 and then asks group members to remove their thumbs and to say out loud the colors on their SCC cards. The SCC cards are placed on the floor in front of them while the leader records participants' colors on the *Stress Away Chart* (see exercise illustration).
    E. The leader reads the directions on back of the SCC and/or reads the Progressive Relaxation sequence while encouraging group members to close their eyes and follow the directions.
    F. Following the completion of the progressive relaxation sequence, group members are asked to once again gently press their thumb on the black square. The leader records participants' colors on the *Stress Away Chart* next to each member's name above or below the diagonal line (see illustration).

Group Discussion:

    • The leader explains how stress affects the body, and how blood is drawn inward causing cold hands when stressed. Therefore, body temperature changes the color of the SCC and the color reflects the degree of stress a person is experiencing. The leader also explains that the simple muscle and mind relaxation techniques they will practice will relieve stress and consequently warm their hands.
    • In this exercise, there should not be any religious symbolism. The exercise is solely based on physiological changes that occur with muscle relaxation.
    • To encourage participation, group members who have learned the relaxation sequence written on the back of each SCC or on the Progressive Relaxation Sequence can take turns leading the sequence.
    • This exercise can be used before each group session to promote increased awareness, cohesiveness, and relaxation. It can be used with all ages and at all stages of development.

---

*SCC can be ordered from BMI, Inc., 2387 East 8 Mile Road, Warren, MI 48091-2403; telephone 1-800-521-4640.

Progressive Relaxation Sequence

Directions: This sequence of progressive muscle relaxation instructions can be used as an alternative to the directions on the *Stress Control Card*. Begin by telling group members that it's important to keep their muscles tensed for 5 to 10 seconds and then to release their tension and allow their muscles to go completely limp. Wait 20 to 30 seconds before shifting to the next muscle group. The group leader should say the following directions in a slow, soft, soothing, repetitive voice.

1. Sit comfortably in a chair or lie in a comfortable position on the floor. (All participants should either sit in a chair or lie on the floor).
2. As you read these instructions, wait 20 to 30 seconds before proceeding to the next muscle group.

   - Wrinkle your forehead and brow. Release, enjoy the relaxed reaction, go completely limp.
   - Tense your eyes and face, squeezing the eyes very tightly. Release, enjoy the relaxed reaction, go completely limp. Let your eyes remain closed.
   - Clench your jaw and press your tongue to the roof of your mouth. Release, enjoy the relaxed reaction, go completely limp.
   - Now tense your neck by pressing your head backwards. Hold, then release, enjoy the relaxed reaction, go completely limp.
   - Then bring your chin to your chest. Hold, then release, enjoy the relaxed reaction, go completely limp.
   - Shrug your shoulders bringing them up toward your ears. Hold, then release, enjoy the relaxed reaction, go completely limp.
   - Make a fist with both your hands. Squeeze, then release, enjoy the relaxed reaction, go completely limp.
   - Take a deep breath, expanding your chest. Hold, now slowly exhale the breath, allowing the chest to relax. Release, enjoy the relaxed reaction, go completely limp.
   - Pull in your stomach muscles. Release, enjoy the relaxed reaction, go completely limp.
   - Tighten your thighs. Release, enjoy the relaxed reaction, go completely limp.
   - Point your toes away from your head, tensing the feet and lower legs. Hold it, then release, enjoy the relaxed reaction, go completely limp.
   - Point toes toward your head. Tense, then release, enjoy the relaxed reaction, go completely limp.

3. Take a full deep breath and hold it for a silent count of 10. When you exhale, let it all out at once, letting your body go completely limp and relaxed.

Stress Away (Sample)

This sample illustrates how a *Stress Away Chart* will look when the group participant's names and colors indicated on their Stress Control Cards (SCCs) are recorded. The color registered on the SCC before the muscle relaxation exercises should be indicated above the diagonal line and below the line after the relaxation sequence.

STRESS AWAY CHART

Black = A lot of stress		Red = A little stress		Green = Normal		Blue = Relaxed		

Date	2/5	2/10	2/15					
Dee	Black / Red	Red / Green	Black / Blue					
Matt	Red / Blue	Black / Green	Red / Red					
Pedro	Green / Blue	Red / Blue	Red / Green					
Lynn	Black / Black	Black / Red						
Joel	Red / Blue	Blue / Blue	Green / Blue					
Ananda	Red / Green	Red / Blue	Green / Green					

Stress Away

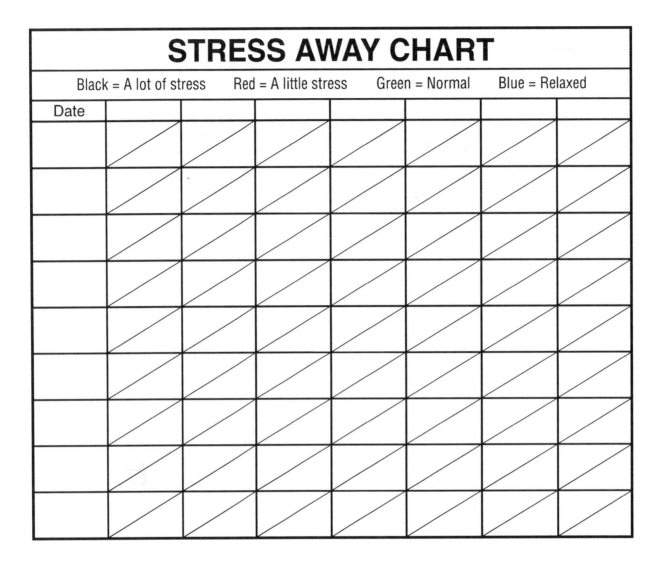

Checking My Self-Esteem

Purpose:

1. To gain awareness of how self-esteem can work for or against you.
2. To help identify areas of self-esteem that are high or low.
3. To develop a greater understanding of how each member can support each other's self-esteem.

Materials:

"Self-Esteem Inventory" activity sheet for each member; writing materials.

Description:

A. The group leader defines self-esteem as follows: "Self-esteem is our sense of self-worth or how we feel about ourselves. It comes from all the thoughts, feelings, and experiences we have about ourselves throughout life. It's being able to meet life's challenges and being worthy of feeling happy."
B. "Self-Esteem Inventory" activity sheets are handed out to each group member. The leader asks participants not to think about each statement too long or to analyze it, but to go with their first response.
C. After about 15 minutes, when activity sheets are completed, ask members to count the negative responses in each category and put that number in the box next to each section.
D. Participants are asked to pair up and take turns discussing their responses to the topics. After a 15-minute discussion, the group leader collects activity sheets and explains that each member will have an opportunity to meet with him or her to find ways of strengthening areas that are low on the "Self-Esteem Inventory" sheet.

Group Discussion:

- It's important to remind participants that this activity is not a test; there are no "right" or "wrong" answers - no high or low scores. This is an opportunity for them to get to know themselves a little better.
- When participants are paired up for discussion, the group leader will circulate throughout the room sitting in on each group to facilitate communication between pairs.
- The best way to get an idea of group members' level of self-esteem is to look at each category separately. If a participant has more than two negative responses in any single category, it's an area where he or she is feeling insecure and one that can be subverting his or her self-esteem. The leader should set time aside to discuss the specific responses individually with the participant and address questions such as: Does he or she feel insecure in a number of areas or just one in particular? What are some specific behaviors he or she can change that will enhance self-esteem?
- This exercise works best with an established group that has developed connections among themselves.

Self-Esteem Inventory

Directions: Read each of the following statements, then circle **T** for true or **F** for false to show whether this is an accurate or inaccurate description of yourself.

PERSONAL POWER

T F   1. I will start projects on my own even if they are challenging.

T F   2. When I make a mistake, I just try to do it right the next time.

T F   3. I know how to deal with stress and pressure.

T F   4. I can assertively communicate my feelings and personal needs.

T F   5. It's pretty easy for me to make decisions and solve problems.

T F   6. I don't always have to get what I want.

UNIQUENESS

T F   1. I enjoy the feeling of being different.

T F   2. I like my body.

T F   3. I like who I am.

T F   4. I enjoy using my imagination and creating things.

T F   5. I often compliment others.

T F   6. When something good happens to me, I feel I deserve it.

MODELS

T F   1. I know what's important to me.

T F   2. I have people in my life that I look up to and respect.

T F   3. I know how to act responsibly.

T F   4. I have goals, and I'm going to achieve them.

T F   5. I've thought about what kind of lifestyle I want to live.

T F   6. I know who to talk to if I have a problem.

CONNECTING RELATIONSHIPS

T F   1. I have at least two friends.

T F   2. I know how my body works and feel good about it.

T F   3. I get along with others.

T F   4. Other people are willing to help me when I need it.

T F   5. I enjoy group activities.

T F   6. I feel close to my family.

Video Self-Modeling

Purpose:

1. To decrease undesirable behaviors and increase appropriate behaviors.
2. To increase self-esteem and positive social skills.

Materials:

Video camera; VCR and TV monitor.

Description:

A. The leader identifies an undesirable behavior that a group member would like to change such as aggressive or passive verbal or physical behavior, general noncompliance, clowning, distractibility, antisocial behavior, overreacting, underreacting, and so on.
B. The leader explains to the participant and other group members that people have changed undesirable behaviors by seeing themselves act in the desired or appropriate way. The participating group member is instructed to act or role-play the desired behavior he or she wants to replace for the undesirable one. For example, if the participant has difficulty attending and listening in a group, he or she will consciously act like he or she is listening to the leader and other group members talking.
C. The group leader videotapes the role-play.
D. Before each group session, the participant watches the video role-play three times before participating in the session.

Group Discussion:

- "Video Self-Modeling" can be a very effective therapeutic exercise with a variety of behaviors as well as emotional problems. I have successfully used this technique in changing a variety of nontolerant and noncompliant behaviors. It has also been a successful agent of change for people who exhibit behaviors associated with Tourette's syndrome, who are selectively mute, behaviorally at risk, or who exhibit low self-image.
- Members are encouraged to discuss why they want to change the inappropriate behavior and what behavior they would like to replace it with. However, the observation of the role-play on tape should be the essential component of this exercise. The video should be viewed for 3 or 4 days consecutively. Thereafter, viewing the video can be used as an intermittent reinforcer. After participants watch themselves acting appropriately, feelings of efficacy become behavior.
- This exercise can be effective with any group, and may be used during all stages of group development.

Making Friends

Purpose:

1. To develop a personal concept of friendship.
2. To increase group members' skills in building and enhancing relationships with peers.

Materials:

One copy of the "Making Friends" activity sheet for each member; pencils; crayons or markers; paper.

Description:

A. The group is asked to think back to their first friendships and how they were developed (e.g., Was it easy or difficult to make a friend, and what made it so?).
B. The leader hands out activity sheets to be filled out by members.
C. After Part I of the activity sheet is completed, members are asked to pair up with someone they have not developed a friendship with and complete Part II of the activity sheet.
D. The leader passes out art materials and asks members to draw a picture of their partner. Underneath the picture they will write a paragraph beginning with "A friend is. . . ." Members are asked to share paragraphs with the group and display their pictures if desired.

Group Discussion:

- The group discussion should also focus on how getting to know another person can be an exciting adventure. The leader should point out that the exchange of information is a very important aspect of making friends. By discovering more about each other's likes and dislikes, partners can begin to establish what is sometimes referred to as a "critical bond" or a greater understanding of each other. Understanding what makes someone angry could increase feelings of tolerance and trust between friends.
- The leader encourages the participants to discuss how problems can be caused in a relationship if there is a lack of information about each other. *For example:* one member becomes quiet when she's upset. It could be pointed out that a friend could either respect her need for being quiet or ask if she wanted to talk about what is upsetting her.
- When pairing up to ask the questions in Part II of the activity sheet, members are encouraged to listen as well as express their personal thoughts openly.
- This exercise can help a group in its beginning stages to feel more at ease with each other. It is especially effective with younger aged participants.

Making Friends
Part I

Directions: Answer the following questions:

1. Do you have a best friend? If so, what is his or her name?

_____

_____

_____

_____

2. How do you make friends?

_____

_____

_____

_____

3. What makes a good friend?

_____

_____

_____

_____

4. Is it better to have a lot of friends or just a few friends? Why?

_____

_____

_____

_____

5. What is there about you that makes your friend like you?

_____

_____

_____

_____

Making Friends
<u>Part II</u>

Directions: Pair up with someone you have not yet developed a friendship with and use the art materials to draw a picture of your partner. After drawing the picture, write a paragraph about what a friend is to you. Use another piece of paper if you need more space to write.

A friend is . . .

Music to My Ears

Purpose:

1. To allow members to identify feelings in a nonthreatening way.
2. To develop group empathy through appreciation for different types of music.

Materials:

A variety of musical cassette tapes (rock, blues, jazz, new age, classical, rap, etc.); cassette tape player; drawing paper; markers; crayons.

Description:

A. A leader can either bring in a variety of music selections or ask group members to bring in their favorite musical tapes. Group members are asked the meaning of "Music expresses the inexpressible." The leader explains that each type of music creates different feelings and thoughts in each of us.
B. While giving out the materials, the leader provides an overview of what this exercise entails, emphasizing expressing one's inner thoughts and feelings in a unique way through "free expression."
C. Members listen to a song from a tape which is played by the leader. They express their feelings and thoughts by drawing, writing, or both, while listening to the music.
D. After playing three or four types of music for 2 or 3 minutes each, the leader asks group members to label each paper with the song title and feelings it evoked.
E. Drawings are displayed and the group discusses each unique expression to the music.

Group Discussion:

- Words from the "Feelings Connection" exercise (Exercise 53, pp. 113-115) can be written on the board for reference. The leader should ask members to refrain from making verbal comments about the music while it is being played, but instead to express their feelings and thoughts on paper. The term "free expression" can be defined as when someone expresses themselves without concern with the outcome. This can be achieved through a variety of expressive media such as drawing, writing, role-playing, singing, and so on.
- Each member is given an opportunity to discuss the drawings or other expressions that illustrate his or her unique thoughts and feelings. Members who share similar feelings to the music should be acknowledged. Members expressing opposite or different feelings should also be acknowledged for their uniqueness, and the group encouraged to accept these differences.
- This exercise is effective with many age groups at all stages of development.

The Prejudice Problem

Purpose:

1. To define and demonstrate understanding of the concept of prejudice.
2. To discuss how prejudice limits self and others.

Materials:

Chalkboard or newsprint; writing materials (optional: VCR, TV).

Description:

A. The group leader reads the following story to the group:

> "Once upon a time there was a girl named Sarah. Sarah was a nice girl who did well in school and had a lot of friends. However, something peculiar about Sarah was that she didn't like pears although she had never eaten one. She was sure that if she did, she would hate the taste. She wasn't exactly sure why she felt this way, she just knew that she did. As Sarah grew older she began to dislike other fruit, and not just any fruit, but other fruit that began with the letter "P." One day she decided she didn't like plums, and then peaches. Pretty soon she disliked *all* food that began with "P," even pumpkin pie! Since foods don't have feelings, Sarah's negative attitude didn't hurt them, but Sarah sure missed out on a lot of good things!"

B. After reading the story, the leader writes the word *prejudice* on the board and asks for a definition.
C. All responses are recorded, and as a group the most appropriate definitions are selected.
D. The group leader facilitates a discussion by relating Sarah's prejudice toward food that begins with the letter "P" to prejudice toward people and groups of people.
E. *Variation:* Form small groups. Each group is asked to create a role-play demonstrating one form of prejudice. The leader can videotape each role-play and then review each one with the entire group. This variation works well with all age groups.

Group Discussion:

- The follow-up group discussion should include these questions:

  ▷ What was Sarah's reason for not liking food that begins with the letter "P"?
  ▷ What do you think might happen if Sarah tried eating a pear and other food that began with "P"?
  ▷ How does ignorance (not getting to know someone or something) contribute to prejudice?
  ▷ How do you think people feel when they experience prejudice from other people?

- This exercise is most effective with groups that are beyond the early stage of development and have established some interpersonal communication skills.

Family Tree

Purpose:

1. To identify lifestyle changes through tracing family histories.
2. To compare participants' lifestyles with their ancestors and identify possible differences.

Materials:

One copy of the "Family Tree" activity sheet for each member; writing materials.

Description:

A. The group leader asks for a definition of "lifestyle." One possible definition is that it is a combination of all things a person does (e.g., home life, job, school, leisure time).
B. While handing out the materials, leaders ask group members to think about their ancestors' occupations, beginning with their parents.
C. After completing the "Family Tree" activity sheets, members divide into small groups to discuss results.
D. *Variation:* Depending on the abilities of the client population, "Family Tree" activity sheets may need to be taken home for assistance and returned the following day to complete this exercise.

Group Discussion:

- Members are asked to share the information on their family tree in their small groups.
- After initial discussion, the group leader asks each member to write on the back of their handout whether their lifestyle differs from that of their ancestors, and to describe why this may be so.
- Group members share what they wrote in their small groups. The leader encourages each group member to listen and compare what they wrote to what others wrote.
- This exercise helps group members increase their understanding and acceptance of individual and family differences. It may be used at any stage in the group's development.

Family Tree

Lifestyles have changed throughout history. Do you agree or disagree with this statement?

Directions: Take a look at your own family history. Chart out your (or a friend's) family tree below. On each leaf, fill in the relative's name, occupation, and birthplace.

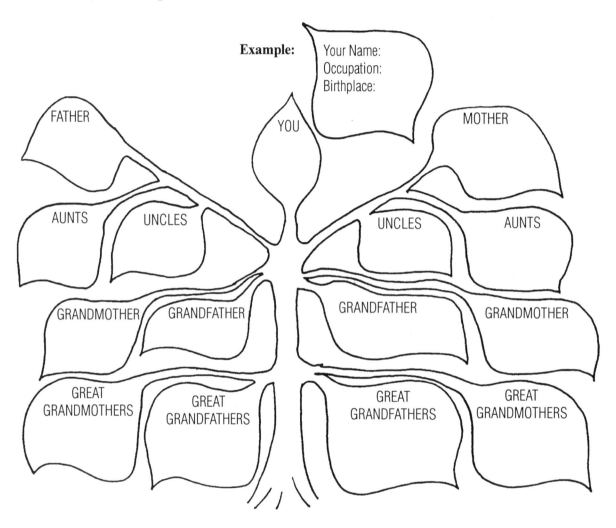

Now that you have the facts in front of you, think about how your lifestyle is different from your ancestors' lifestyles. Write your opinion below.

Unity in Our Uniqueness

Purpose:

1. To increase appreciation for group diversity.
2. To develop awareness of one's unique facial qualities within a group.

Materials:

Mirrors; drawing paper; pencils; India ink; paint brushes; crayons or magic markers; tape; scissors.

Description:

A. The leader begins the exercise by pointing out that as no two snowflakes are exactly alike, there are also no two faces which look exactly alike. The question is asked, "What would it be like if, in fact, everyone looked the same?"
B. The materials are distributed, and the leader asks members to look in a mirror and make an approximate life-size drawing of their faces.
C. Each member is given a brush and India ink to outline their features. Magic markers or crayons are then used to add color to hair, eyes, and so on.
D. Faces are cut out and displayed on a bulletin board or wall by overlapping them, creating a "group look."
E. *Variation:* Have group members pair up and draw each other's face without using mirrors.

Group Discussion:

- Some group members might feel hesitant to draw themselves due to poor body image or lack of confidence in artistic skills. The group leader should emphasize the importance of trying to create a similarity to one's face but not to be concerned with realism. Facial features such as blue eyes, curly hair, eyeglasses, and so on, should be represented.
- When faces are displayed together, each member can give a short response to the group about feelings the image may evoke and why.
- This exercise can build a group's identity and can be successfully done with a variety of age groups at all stages of the group's development.

My Own Uniqueness

Purpose:

1. To recognize personal unique qualities.
2. To increase awareness of other group members' unique and similar qualities.
3. To develop an appreciation of each other's uniqueness.

Materials:

One copy of the "Uniqueness" activity sheet for each member; writing materials.

Description:

A. The leader talks about the different things that make someone unique. The group is asked to also give examples.
B. While members are given a copy of the "Uniqueness" activity sheet, they are reminded that their responses to the incomplete sentences are true to them and cannot be right or wrong.
C. Members are asked to form small groups of three or four and share their responses on each incomplete sentence.
D. *Variation:* Each member can check three responses that they really like about themselves and discuss why in a large or small group.

Group Discussion:

- When the leader is talking about uniqueness, these thoughts should be included: "No one else is exactly like you - you are unique. Part of what makes you unique is the way you express yourself, the way you think and communicate." Group members are then asked to give an example of a personal unique quality. The group leader helps to highlight the personal qualities expressed by each member.
- In the small groups, the leader checks to see if members are sharing not only differences but also similarities.
- Groups in all stages of formation can benefit from this exercise.

Uniqueness

Your "Uniqueness" can mean some kinds of differences when compared to someone else.

Directions: To understand and explore more about your personal unique qualities use the "I" statements and complete each sentence.

I am _____

I will _____

I can _____

I feel _____

I think _____

I know _____

I was _____

I have _____

I don't _____

I wish _____

I should _____

I could _____

I want _____

After sharing these answers with other group members, answer the following questions:

How many of your responses were unique? _____

How many were shared by others? _____

Sharing My Special Talents

Purpose:

1. To describe each member's unique abilities and talents.
2. To acknowledge the abilities and talents of other members.
3. To demonstrate understanding of the concept "strength in diversity."

Materials:

Copies of the activity sheet "My Special Talents" for each participant; writing materials.

Description:

A. The group leader introduces the activity by asking group members to think about talents or "gifts" that they possess.
B. Leader distributes the activity sheet "My Special Talents." Participants write down as many of their own talents as they can think of.
C. When participants have completed, the leader asks them to review their sheets and circle one talent that they would feel comfortable describing to their peers.
D. Members are then asked to form small groups of four to six and take turns sharing their thoughts and feelings about their identified talent.

Group Discussion:

- When asking members to think about a talent they possess, the leader explains that a talent or gift is a special ability, like the ability to play a musical instrument, to draw pictures, or speak another language.
- It's also important to explain that some people have a talent in math, science, or history; others are talented at making friends or playing a sport. Describe to the participants two or three talents or gifts that *you* possess.
- While the group members are working on filling out their activity sheets, the leader circulates and offers help and suggestions as needed.
- After giving each group approximately 10 minutes to discuss their talents, the leader asks these questions:

  ▷ How are our gifts and talents the same? How are they different?
  ▷ What would it be like if everyone had exactly the same gifts and talents?

- This exercise works especially well in the beginning stages of the group's formation.

My Special Talents

Directions: After filling in your name, write down as many of your special talents that you can think of. *For example:* I can bake bread, or play the recorder, or skateboard, and so on.

My name is _____ , and I bring these special talents to my group:

1. _____

_____

_____

_____

2. _____

_____

_____

_____

3. _____

_____

_____

_____

4. _____

_____

_____

_____

5. _____

_____

_____

_____

What Do I Believe?

Purpose:

    1. To help identify personal values and beliefs.

    2. To increase understanding and acceptance of others' beliefs.

Materials:

    Newspaper; writing materials; "Belief List" activity sheet for each member.

Description:

    A. The group leader reads an article from a newspaper that addresses a controversial issue (e.g., capital punishment, abortion, etc.). The leader explains that issues such as the one just read are often decided based on people's personal beliefs.

    B. "Belief List" activity sheets are handed out to each group member. The group leader chooses a topic from the list to be discussed and asks members to write their personal belief about the chosen topic.

    C. Participants are asked to pair up and take turns discussing their responses to the topic.

    D. After discussion in pairs, members are asked to share responses in a large group. Time permitting, the group leader can choose another topic from the "Belief List" and repeat the entire process.

    E. *Variation:* Participants can choose a topic to discuss when they pair up with a partner. Additional "belief" questions can be generated by group members.

Group Discussion:

- When sitting in pairs, each member is given approximately 2 minutes to discuss his or her personal belief.
- Each member is encouraged to listen to his or her partner without judging whether the partner's belief is right or wrong.
- In the large group, participants summarize what they feel they have learned about their beliefs as well as those of others through this activity.
- This exercise can be entertaining as well as revealing, depending upon the composition of the group. It's important to encourage individual participation in the group discussion.
- This exercise can be used with a variety of groups that have already established some rapport.

Belief List

Directions: In the space provided below, write your personal beliefs under the topic being discussed.

1. Is there a God?

_____

_____

2. Is democracy the best form of government?

_____

_____

3. Do I believe in premarital sex?

_____

_____

4. Is it right to kill animals for food?

_____

_____

5. What do I think about interracial marriages?

_____

_____

6. Should smoking be banned from public places?

_____

_____

7. Is it ever okay to hit someone as a means of discipline?

_____

_____

8. Is homework needed?

_____

_____

9. What should the drinking age be?

_____

_____

10. What do I think about tattoos?

_____

What Do I See?

Purpose:

1. To create individual drawing interpretations starting from the same set of lines.
2. To increase understanding of each person's uniqueness.
3. To recognize that having different perceptions does not automatically make one person right and another wrong.

Materials:

One copy of the activity sheet "What Do I See?" for each member; art materials.

Description:

A. Group members are given a copy of the activity sheet and asked to look at the lines for a few moments, allowing the lines to suggest a picture in their imaginations.
B. Art materials are distributed and participants are directed to recall the picture in their imagination and draw it, using the lines already on the page.
C. At the conclusion of their drawings, ask each group member to share their pictures.
D. Leader facilitates a follow-up discussion, emphasizing differences in perception and interpretation.

Group Discussion:

- While group members are drawing their personal interpretations on the activity sheet, encourage independent work and discourage talking during this process.
- The group leader should assure participants that there is no right or wrong way to complete the activity, but that everyone must rely on his or her own creativity and perceptions based on imagination.
- The follow-up discussion should include these questions:

  ▷ Were any of our pictures "right" or "wrong"? Why?
  ▷ If we all saw the lines differently, what other things in life do you think we might see differently?
  ▷ Why is it important to understand that people have a right to see things in their own ways?

- This exercise is effective with groups in any stage of development.

What Do I See?

Directions: Look at the lines and shapes that are on this page for a few moments, allowing them to create a picture in your mind. Then close your eyes for a few seconds "seeing" the picture you've created. When ready, draw the picture you created in your imagination.

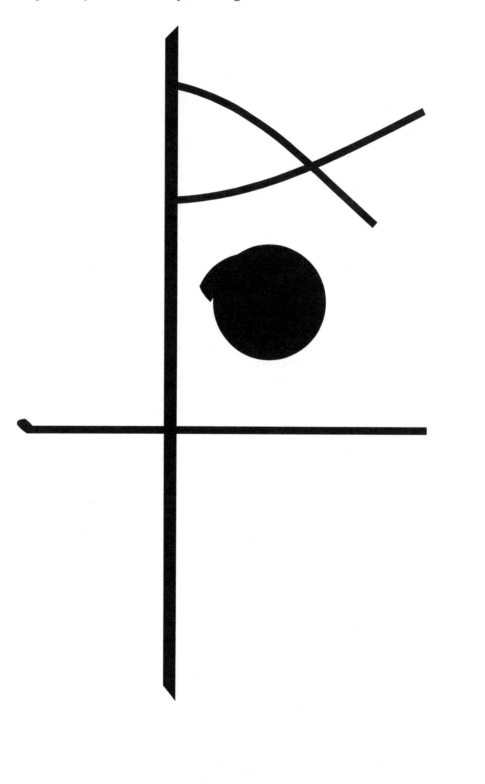

The Emotional Pie

Purpose:

1. To define different feelings one might experience throughout a day.
2. To increase awareness of possible causes of and consequences to one's feelings.
3. To develop group cohesion through mutual self-disclosure.

Materials:

Newsprint; magic markers; tape; "Pie Chart" activity sheet.

Description:

A. The group leader explains: "We all go through many emotions and feelings throughout the day but are rarely aware of what they are or why they are caused. *For example:* When I came to work today I realized that I was feeling frustrated. When I walked out to my car before coming to work I almost slipped on the ice. Did that cause my frustration?"

B. On a piece of newsprint taped to the wall, the leader draws a large circle and divides the circle into pie-like sections which represent the feelings experienced during the day (see illustration).

C. The leader draws four or five colors on the top of the newsprint that represent different feelings (e.g., red for anger, blue for relaxed, orange for frustrated, etc.). Each section of the pie is colored the feeling experienced. The group leader then briefly explains what causes each feeling.

D. Newsprint and markers are passed out to members sitting in small groups of three or four. They are asked to create their own "Emotional Pies" by drawing a circle and picking colors that represent feelings (writing feelings next to each color). Then they divide circle into sections representing feelings experienced throughout the day.

E. After completing the exercise, the leader displays the drawings by taping them on the wall in a line.

Group Discussion:

• Members describe their personal "Emotional Pies" to the group and tell what caused each feeling represented by a different color.

• This discussion may evolve into the sharing of how feelings can create positive and negative attitudes throughout the day.

• The group leader can choose to ask members to make an emotional pie each day for a week to see if reactions to emotions change once people become more aware of what they are feeling.

• This exercise can be used with a variety of groups whose members have already established some interpersonal skills.

Example of Completed Pie Chart

Angry = Red ◎   Happy = Yellow ◎
Tired = Blue ●   Frustrated = Orange ◉

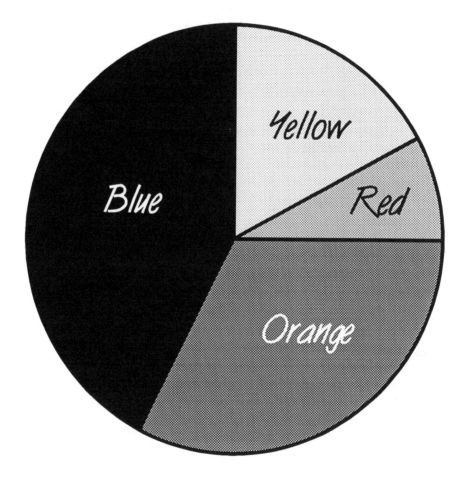

Pie Chart

Directions: Write your feelings and the colors you chose to represent your feelings below.

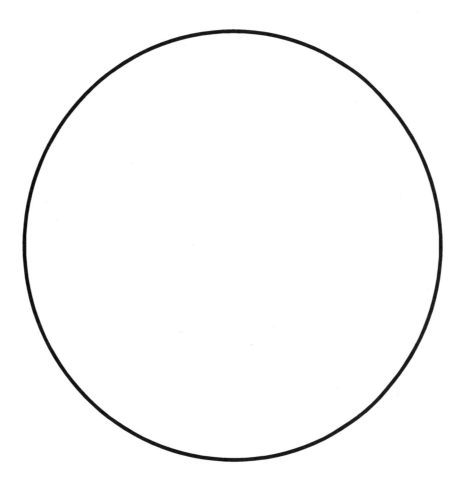

Team Puzzle

Purpose:

1. To encourage cooperative problem solving among group members.
2. To identify specific cooperative and competitive behaviors and describe how they affect completion of a group task.
3. To incorporate feedback into self-evaluation.

Materials:

Construction paper or art board (one color only); scissors; envelopes.

Description:

A. Group leader will need to cut three 8" x 8" squares of construction paper into three to five smaller puzzle pieces (see illustration) for each group. The groups then receive all of these pieces in a single envelope.
B. Members are asked to form into groups of four. Each group is seated around a table and selects one member to be its observer. It is explained that the observer's job is to notice specific cooperative versus competitive behaviors, any conflicts that occur, and how they are resolved.
C. The leader distributes approximately the same number of puzzle pieces randomly among the three players and reads aloud the following rules of play:

- Your task is to assemble three squares of EQUAL size.
- There will be no talking, pointing, or other nonverbal communication between group members.
- If a player needs a puzzle part to help complete his or her puzzle, it must be passed to him or her. In order for this to happen, each group member needs to observe each other's puzzles and try to help complete each other's puzzles without taking or asking each other for a puzzle piece.

Group Discussion:

- At the conclusion of play, the observer is asked to describe such things as how well the group worked together; who shared puzzle parts and who did not, whether members concentrated on one partner's puzzle or all three, cooperative versus competitive behaviors, and any conflicts that arose during the exercise and how they were resolved.
- After all groups are finished (approximately 15 minutes should be allowed), a discussion can include what was learned from the observers, and what was learned from the experience.
- This exercise works well with groups whose members are insightful and capable of abstract reasoning. Depending on the cognitive maturity of the group's members, the leader should decide on the number of puzzle pieces (3-5) for each group.

Team Puzzle

Directions: These puzzle pictures can be cut out or used as stencils for the construction paper.

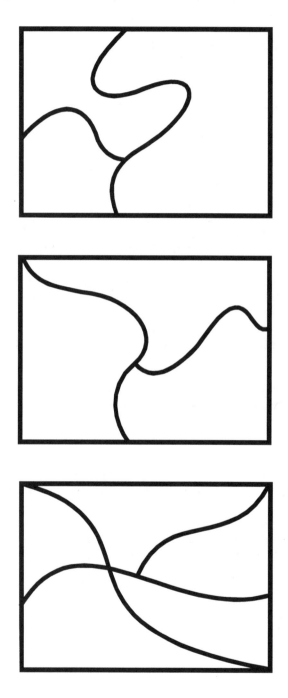

Close Cooperation

Purpose:

1. To define and develop a better understanding of the word *cooperate*.
2. To describe the benefits of close cooperation with others to achieve a goal.

Materials:

One copy of the activity sheet, "Working Together" for each participant; chalkboard or newsprint; writing materials.

Description:

A. The group leader writes the word *cooperate* on the board and asks group members what it means to cooperate with another person, writing their responses on the board.
B. The leader reminds the group members of specific times when they were asked to work together to complete an activity or task.
C. The group is asked to answer the question, "What did you gain by working together cooperatively?" Answers are recorded on the board.
D. The following potential benefits of working cooperatively with another person are addressed. When people get together, they:

   - Save time.
   - Think of more solutions to a problem.
   - Can have fun.
   - Get to know each other.

E. The activity sheets are distributed. Members are given a few minutes to complete the sheet. If time permits, they can share what they have written in small groups of two to four.

Group Discussion:

- When group members are asked to define the word *cooperate*, the leader should accept all contributions, writing key words and phrases on the board (e.g., together, save time, fun, etc.).
- A group discussion should include these questions:

   ▷ What are some ways that you cooperate with others at home? work? recreation?
   ▷ What happens when one person in a group is uncooperative?
   ▷ If you had an uncooperative person in your group, what could you do?

- This exercise has worked well at the beginning of the formation of a group. Depending on the maturity of each member, the leader will need to encourage openness and responses to questions by giving examples.

Working Together

Directions: Write two or three sentences that describe what the word *cooperating* means to you. Below are some words that can be incorporated into your sentences. Feel free to use other words, too.

fun	share	solutions
helpful	team	communicate
together	think	support

To me, *cooperating* means _____

_____

_____

_____

_____

_____

_____

_____

_____

When finished, in the space below, write about a time when you successfully cooperated with someone to reach a goal.

_____

_____

_____

_____

_____

_____

_____

_____

_____

_____

_____

Anthology of Short Stories

Purpose:

1. To increase the experience of group cooperation.
2. To share responsibility in order to complete a task.

Materials:

One copy of "Our Story" activity sheet for each small group; writing materials; construction paper; crayons or markers; stapler.

Description:

A. The leader prepares the group for this exercise by asking the participants these questions: "If you could write a book, what would it be about? Fiction or nonfiction? Drama? Mystery? Romance? Thriller?"
B. Participants are divided into groups of four and told to decide on a theme for a story they will cooperatively write (e.g., sports, dating, vampires, etc.).
C. Each group is given a copy of the "Our Story" activity sheet and one member from each group is told to write their theme on top of the page. Each group member takes a turn answering one of the who, when, where, and what questions. Answers need to be written in full sentences.
D. A member is chosen to design a cover for the entire group's stories or the anthology of stories. When activity sheets are completed, the stories are stapled together.
E. The leader reads the completed stories to the group and facilitates a discussion.
F. *Variations:*

    ✓ Depending on the size of the group, participants can write a sentence each and create a story that is passed on from group member to member until completed.
    ✓ For participants who have difficulty expressing their ideas by writing them, they can take turns speaking into a tape recorder and then listen to their cooperative story.

Group Discussion:

- Each group should be given 5 to 10 minutes to describe a theme for their story. The leader can suggest writing down all suggestions and then taking a quick vote to decide which one should be used.
- The leader may need to assign each group member a question to answer on the activity sheet. This will depend on the maturity and ability of each of its members to work cooperatively. After reading each group's story, the discussion should include: How did the groups work together? What were the challenges? Was it enjoyable or frustrating? Why?
- This exercise is effective with groups that may need help with development of cooperation and interpersonal communication skills. It may be too complex for participants whose language and writing skills are severely delayed.
- This exercise is most successful with groups that have established group cooperation strategies.

Our Story

_____

Story Theme

Directions: Now that you have decided on a theme for your story, take turns answering the following questions. Try to use your imagination and have fun!

WHO is this story about?

_____
_____
_____
_____
_____

WHEN did it take place?

_____
_____
_____
_____
_____

WHERE did it happen?

_____
_____
_____
_____
_____

WHAT happened?

_____
_____
_____
_____
_____

Co-Op City

Purpose:

1. To increase group cooperation.
2. To develop understanding of the group decision-making process.
3. To promote feedback about perceptions of group process.

Materials:

Clay; large piece of plywood or masonite; clay working tools; newsprint or blackboard; markers.

Description:

A. The leader begins this exercise by asking the group to think about how they would design a village or city that would support cooperative living.
B. On the board, the leader writes suggestions from members concerning the various parts of the cooperative city. Included could be types of buildings, bridges, parks, and so on.
C. Before the leader gives out materials, the group is asked to decide how they will work together toward the goal of constructing the city.
D. The leader gives out materials and encourages members to communicate their ideas as they construct the cooperative city out of clay on the plywood board.
E. Members evaluate process and results.

Group Discussion:

- The leader helps members explore the process of working together toward a common goal by asking questions such as:

  ▷ How were decisions made?
  ▷ What was difficult about working together?
  ▷ Enjoyable?
  ▷ Are you satisfied with the results? Why?

- This exercise is effective and fun when used in the early stages of group development to facilitate group processing and identity.

Making a Decision

Purpose:

1. To become aware of group members' own decision-making process.
2. To increase understanding of how to successfully arrive at a decision and its consequences.

Materials:

Paper; writing materials; chalkboard or newsprint; chalk.

Description:

A. The leader tells a story of a decision made recently in his or her own life. *For example:* "Recently, I made a decision to sell my car and buy a new one. In some ways it was an easy decision to make, but in others, a difficult one. Buying a new car versus a used one has its disadvantages as well as advantages. I want you to think about a decision you've made recently."

B. Each member is given a piece of paper and pencil and asked to write one decision they recently made.

C. Members are divided into small groups of three to five each and asked to take turns reading their decisions to each other.

D. The group leader then asks each member to answer discussion questions written on the board.

E. After approximately 10 minutes of discussion, a volunteer from each small group shares decision and answers to questions with large group.

Group Discussion:

- Questions each member is asked to answer are:

  ▷ What prompted you to make that decision?
  ▷ Were there any alternatives to the decision you made?
  ▷ What are the consequences of the decision you made?

- The group leader encourages other members to discuss other ways the decisions could have been made. But members are reminded of the importance of not judging whether the decision was a "good or bad" one. That would be up to the member who made the decision to decide. This exercise can be done with a variety of groups beyond the early stage of development.
- This exercise should precede the "Solving a Problem" exercise (Exercise 40, pp. 85-86).

Solving a Problem

Purpose:

1. To develop skills necessary for solving problems.
2. To increase problem solving among small and large groups of people.
3. To recognize and understand each other's needs.

Materials:

One copy of "Steps Toward Solving a Problem" activity sheet for each group member; writing materials; newsprint or chalkboard.

Description:

A. The leader explores with the group how problems that need to be solved arise continuously.
B. While giving out materials the leader asks the members to think about a decision they've made in the past couple of days or a problem they needed to solve.
C. The leader writes on the board each step to making a decision, referring to the Problem Solving Format (see below).
D. Group members fill out exercise sheet. Group is divided into pairs. Members take turns sharing their answers and evaluation of their decision with their partner.
E. A volunteer from the group is asked to share their answers with whole group.
F. *Variation:* Members role-play a problem they are having with a peer and use problem-solving questions as a guide for resolving conflict.

Group Discussion:

- While participants are in pairs discussing their answers with each partner, the group leader should listen in on each group and give encouragement and clarification to the process when needed.
- ***Problem Solving Format:***

  ▷ *What is the problem?* One of the hardest parts of decision making may be stating exactly what the problem is in the first place.
  ▷ *What are the alternatives? Resources?* Once the problem has been defined, make a list of all the possible alternatives to solving the problem. Include a list of *resources* (money, friends, talent, etc.) that can be used to help solve the problem.
  ▷ *Analyze the alternatives.* Look at each alternative closely. Which one is best?
  ▷ *Decide.* The decision can now be easily (hopefully) made.
  ▷ *Evaluate the decision.* Making the decision is not the end of the process. Now you have to look back to see if that decision worked out well for you. What have you learned? What will you do next time? Is this decision safe? Fair to others?

- This exercise can be used with a variety of age groups.

Steps Toward
Solving a Problem

Directions: Fill in answers to the following questions.

1. What is the problem? (Pick a problem large or small that needs to be solved.)

    _____

    _____

    _____

2. What are the alternatives? (List them.)

    _____

    _____

    _____

    Resources? (List them.)

    _____

    _____

    _____

3. Analyze the alternatives. (List best alternatives and state why they are the best choices.)

    _____

    _____

    _____

4. Decide. (Pick the best choice.)

    _____

    _____

    _____

5. Evaluate the decision. (Did it work? Why? Why not?)

    _____

    _____

    _____

Negative, Positive, And Neutral Mind

Purpose:

    1. To increase self-awareness.
    2. To identify three types of thought patterns.
    3. To promote problem-solving skills.

Materials:

    "Negative, Positive, and Neutral Mind (NPN)" activity sheet for each group member; blackboard or newsprint; writing materials; half-filled glass of water.

Description:

    A. The leader writes on the board "Negative, Positive, and Neutral" and explains that one way to look at how we think is that we have *three minds,* the negative, positive, and neutral minds. The group leader defines each "mind" by saying, "The *negative* mind warns you of a potential problem, the *positive* mind looks at the good side of things, and the *neutral* mind looks at both the negative and positive and then makes an objective or neutral decision. After I tell you this personal story I want you to tell me which was my negative, positive, and neutral mind" (see "Group Discussion" for story).

    B. After telling the story, the group leader puts a half-filled glass of water on a table and asks, "Point your thumb up if you think this glass is half full and down if you think it's half empty." The leader explains that there is no correct answer, that it depends on how you want to think about it.

    C. Leader passes out the "NPN Mind" activity sheets and asks each group member to complete the four scenarios.

    D. As participants complete their activity sheets, they are paired up with another person to compare and discuss answers. All participants then form a large group and discuss which "mind" supports their needs.

    E. *Variation:* Group members are divided into groups of three. Each participant in a group takes turns writing the response for either the negative, positive, or neutral mind. When all scenarios are completed, the large group discusses members' experiences in writing their responses.

Group Discussion:

    • An example of a personal story told by the group leader will illustrate the three minds: "Yesterday my friend asked me if I wanted to go skiing. Part of me thought 'that's a great idea, I need to exercise!' But another part of me said, 'my knee has been bothering me lately and maybe I shouldn't ski anymore.' Then a third voice in my head said, 'let's see, you haven't skied in a while and need the exercise. If you don't push yourself too hard and only ski for a few hours, it should be all right.' "

    • When participants pair up to discuss their answer, it's important that they understand not to criticize each other but instead to try and understand the different ways we often approach a problem and what works best for us.

Negative, Positive, and Neutral Mind

Directions: Read the following scenarios and write the possible Negative, Positive, and Neutral (NPN) Mind responses.

Scenario #1
You have been invited to go on vacation to Florida for a week with your grandparents.

Negative Mind: _____

_____

Positive Mind: _____

Neutral Mind: _____

_____

Scenario #2
There is a movie you want to see that's on TV at 9:00 p.m. during a school night.

Negative Mind: _____

_____

Positive Mind: _____

Neutral Mind: _____

_____

Scenario #3
Your friend wants to introduce you to a possible date from another town.

Negative Mind: _____

_____

Positive Mind: _____

Neutral Mind: _____

_____

Scenario #4
You've been offered a baby-sitting job every Friday night for 6 months.

Negative Mind: _____

_____

Positive Mind: _____

Neutral Mind: _____

_____

Is That Good Advice?

Purpose:

1. To assist in differentiating between helpful and nonhelpful advice.
2. To increase problem-solving skills.

Materials:

One photocopy of "Is That Good Advice?" activity sheet for each member; writing materials; blackboard or newsprint.

Description:

A. An initial discussion focuses on times when others' input might be beneficial before making a decision. Examples could include buying a gift or how to settle a dispute with another person. It is pointed out to members that sometimes they can benefit from others' advice and sometimes not.
B. Participants are asked to sit in pairs and are each given an activity sheet. Each member is instructed to read the "Life Situation" and take turns writing what might be helpful and not helpful advice.
C. When completed, all participants sit in a circle and take turns sharing their responses.
D. The leader asks participants to write in their own "Life Situation" on the activity sheet and then fill in the advice columns. Group discusses responses.

Group Discussion:

- The group members listen to each participant's response to the advice columns and then are encouraged to express their thoughts and feelings concerning what makes advice beneficial or not.
- The leader facilitates the discussion by recording the group's responses on the board.
- This exercise is especially useful with groups that may need help with problem-solving and critical-thinking skills.
- This exercise can be effective with all types of groups. It is particularly useful with adolescents and preadolescents.

Is That Good Advice?

Life Situation	Helpful Advice	Not Helpful Advice
1. You want to make some extra spending money but also need to focus on homework.		
2. Your brother/sister takes your personal possessions without asking and usually forgets to return them.		
3. You want to talk to a girl/boy in your school but are not sure if she/he likes you.		
4. You notice someone shoplifting in a department store.		
5. A friend tells you his father always hits him.		

Menu Please!

Purpose:

1. To increase understanding and practice of appropriate restaurant etiquette.
2. To practice skills that promote confidence and self-evaluation of behavior in a restaurant.

Materials:

Menus; table and chairs; silverware; plates; salt and pepper; video camera; newsprint or blackboard.

Description:

A. The group leader asks group members questions pertaining to restaurant etiquette and writes answers on board.
B. Following the discussion, ask for volunteers to role-play a waiter or waitress while others take turns acting as the customers.
C. The group leader videotapes the role-play between group members. Each role-play should take no longer than 10 to 15 minutes.
D. The group members are asked to view the videotape of their role-play and evaluate their performance by discussing what they saw.

Group Discussion:

- When discussing restaurant etiquette with group members, include the following questions:

  ▷ How do you order from a menu?
  ▷ Who should order first?
  ▷ What silverware do you use when there is more than one fork and spoon?
  ▷ How do you use the napkin?
  ▷ When do you begin to eat?
  ▷ How do you ask for condiments that are not in your immediate reach?
  ▷ How do you get the waiter or waitress?

- When discussing these questions, give members an opportunity to express their thoughts without correction from the leader or other group members. The group leader keeps track of answers, then reviews them, making needed corrections.
- While viewing the videotape, the leader should stop at each moment a specific skill needs to be evaluated (e.g., using the napkin). Group members can then volunteer to talk about what they observed. The leader can refer back to the initial questions and the correct answers as members discuss what they observed.
- This exercise is effective with younger (mental and chronological) ages and at all stages of group development.

Protect Yourself

Purpose:

1. To increase personal knowledge and awareness of protective skills at home and in the community.
2. To promote interaction by sharing viewpoints.

Materials:

One "Protect Yourself" activity sheet copied for each member; writing materials.

Description:

A. The leader asks participants why they think parents often tell their children not to take money from strangers or get into a car with someone they don't know. The leader explains that if members understood the reasons for not getting in a car with a stranger, they have gained knowledge that will keep them safe; or protective skills.
B. After discussion, the leader passes out an activity sheet to members and asks them to work either in pairs or individually to fill them out.
C. When finished, members are encouraged to take turns sharing answers in the large group.

Group Discussion:

- The group leader should be aware of emphasizing a sense of empowerment around safety and personal protection skills with clients, as some of these questions might bring up fearful inner responses. The responses might be felt due to a negative past experience or an imagined one that was created by possibly watching TV or a movie. Explaining that knowledge of what to do and not to do in all situations involving safety will only help them feel more in control and safe.
- The use of role-play is an option that can assist each participant in the understanding of the various protective actions. By acting out appropriate responses, participants can experience its effect on others as well as themselves. It's also important to encourage positive responses from other group members when role-players practice skills. *An example is:* "a stranger bothering you in a movie." Participants role-play getting out of their seat and telling an "usher" what the problem is.
- It's important that the group leader encourages students to express their feelings and ask questions regarding the protective actions they chose.
- This exercise can be successfully done with a variety of age groups.

Protect Yourself

Directions: To help you identify what you already know and what you might need to understand. Read the statements 1 to 15. As you read each statement, find the correct behavior under "Protective Actions" and write the letter in the blank.

Statements

_____ 1. Someone is following you in a car.

_____ 2. You see a friend hitchhike a ride.

_____ 3. A stranger telephones when you are at home alone.

_____ 4. You ride your bike to the store.

_____ 5. You have birthday money.

_____ 6. You are baby-sitting and the child gets hurt.

_____ 7. You must take your house key to school.

_____ 8. A stranger says that he or she has been sent to take you home from school.

_____ 9. A stranger bothers you in a movie.

_____ 10. Your bike has been stolen.

_____ 11. You have just witnessed a crime.

_____ 12. You are playing in an empty building.

_____ 13. You need to call for help, and there is no telephone book.

_____ 14. You have just gotten a new jacket.

_____ 15. Your friend wants to shoplift.

Protective Actions

a. Call parents, neighbors, or police.

b. You are vulnerable to crime.

c. Move and tell an usher.

d. You are the victim and should call the police.

e. Mark it for identification before you wear it.

f. Remember what you saw and report it to police.

g. Dial "0" or 911.

h. Turn and run in the opposite direction.

i. Copy down the license number and call police.

j. Tell them your parents are busy and to please call back.

k. Leave it at home in a safe place.

l. Wear it inside clothing.

m. Call parent to make sure.

n. Lock it properly.

o. Try to talk your friend out of it. If you can't, do not go with him or her.

Perfectly Imperfect

Purpose:

1. To develop a positive self-image and acceptance of one's unique qualities.
2. To explore how "not perfect" labels become individual truths.

Materials:

One copy of "Perfectly Imperfect" activity sheet for each member; writing materials.

Description:

A. The group leader asks participants to think about these questions: "Can you think about a part of you about which you've been given the message, either directly or indirectly, that it is not perfect? For instance, many movie stars get plastic surgery to change the shape of their noses, chins, breasts, and so on. Why?"

B. As the leader passes out "Perfectly Imperfect" activity sheets, the participants are told they will now get an opportunity to explore their thoughts and feelings about the issue of "looking perfect." They fill out activity sheets individually.

C. Group members are asked to sit in pairs to discuss their answers.

D. After 5 to 10 minutes of discussion time, participants are brought together and volunteers are asked to share an answer with the large group until questions 1 to 5 on the activity sheet are addressed.

E. *Variation:* Ask participants to look through popular entertainment and teen magazines. Photographs and articles can then be used as a catalyst for discussion about the messages given to the consumer about "perfect" physical qualities.

Group Discussion:

- During the group discussion, the leader should stress the importance of deciding for oneself whether to accept the way one looks versus reacting to external pressure from media and peers.
- Because this exercise is introspective, it works best with a group beyond the initial stage of development.

Perfectly Imperfect
Activity Sheet

Perfectly Imperfect

Directions: To help you identify feelings and thoughts about your "unique imperfections," answer these questions.

1. What are ways people determine what might be perfect as far as physical features?

   _____

   _____

   _____

   _____

2. Are there any parts of your body that you think are not perfect? If so, what are they?

   _____

   _____

   _____

   _____

3. Can you think back to when you "got the message" from the media (i.e., TV, magazines) or anyone else that these parts of your body are not perfect? If so, describe your experience(s).

   _____

   _____

   _____

   _____

4. How about imperfect behavior? Do you have any? How do you know?

   _____

   _____

   _____

   _____

5. Can you feel OK with these so-called physical and behavioral imperfections? Why? Why not?

   _____

   _____

   _____

   _____

Peer Pressure

Purpose:

1. To examine different ways of dealing with peer pressure conflicts.
2. To share responsibility in order to complete an activity.

Materials:

One copy of a role-play situation from the "Peer Pressure" activity sheet for each group member; paper; scissors; writing materials (optional: video camera, VCR, and TV monitor).

Description:

A. A brief discussion is initiated about peer pressure. Members give examples of when they have experienced peer pressure, how they typically react to it, and why.
B. Group participants are divided into three groups. Each group is given a cut-out copy of role-play situation one, two, or three and a blank piece of paper.
C. The leader asks each group to read their role-play situations and decide on one ending scenario for the role-play. Then ending should be written down on a piece of paper.
D. Each group is asked to act out their situation and its ending in front of the large group. The group leader assists each group with their choice of actors.
E. After each role-play, the group discusses endings.
F. *Variation:* Videotape each group role-playing their situations separately, then play them back for group discussion.

Group Discussion:

- Members are encouraged to cooperatively decide whatever ending they feel is appropriate before role-playing the situations.
- The group leader should include the following information while discussing peer pressure: "In peer pressure situations you are likely to experience both positive and negative feelings. It's important to pay attention to your feelings so that you can make the right decision. When you are with your friends, try to express how you really feel without hurting anyone's feelings. But you also want to be true to your values or what you believe in."
- This exercise is effective at all stages of group development.

Peer Pressure

Directions: Each group is given one cut-out copy of Role-Play Situation One, Two, or Three. Read each activity sheet scenario and decide on an ending.

Role-Play Situation One: Shoplifting

Shawn, 16 years old, has just been hired as a clerk in a local music store. He had been trying to get the job for several months in order to add to the income at home and is anxious to succeed. The store's owner emphasizes over and over how important it is for Shawn to keep his eyes open for shoplifters. The owner keeps a meticulous count of the inventory and cash register receipts. In fact, Shawn only had a chance at the job because his predecessor was fired for negligence.

During the second week on the job, Shawn's friend Lucy comes into the store. Shawn watches as Lucy slips two tapes under her coat. Lucy then approaches Shawn at the cash register to pay for yet another cassette tape. Shawn whispers to Lucy that she should return the two tapes she has stolen. Lucy responds with a wink and a snicker.

How should Shawn deal with this situation?

Role-Play Situation Two: Going With the Crowd

At summer camp, many of the teens smoke without the camp's or their parents' knowledge, even though the camp forbids smoking and will send home anyone who is caught smoking. One day, three girls are sitting behind their cabin while everyone else is inside resting. Susan, a very shy girl, sits with them, not only because she really likes the girls but also because she desperately wants to be liked and accepted by the others. The other girls start smoking and offer Susan a cigarette. Susan has never smoked before. She is afraid to break camp rules, and she really doesn't want to smoke. However, she knows these girls will laugh at her and reject her if she refuses.

What should Susan do?

Role-Play Situation Three: Cheating

Velma is taking a final exam in her English class and has prepared diligently for the test. As she turns to the second page of the exam, Ron, her boyfriend who is sitting next to her, whispers that he has studied the wrong material. He is frantic, but is sure he can get the answers from Velma.

Velma's grade in this class is very important to her, because she hopes to qualify for a substantial scholarship that is being offered by the local bank. She knows that if she is caught cheating, she will be instantly disqualified. But she also knows Ron is in danger of failing the class, and she is frightened of his reaction if she refuses to help him. Ron is easily the most popular boy in his class, and Velma spent half the year just getting him to notice her. She has no doubt that, if she doesn't help him cheat, Ron will not only drop her, but will degrade and belittle her to the rest of the school.

What should Velma do?

Human Needs

Purpose:

1. To identify the five basic human needs described by Abraham Maslow.
2. To describe personal behaviors that represent the five basic needs.
3. To increase group understanding of individual member's needs and ways they can be fulfilled.

Materials:

One copy of "Human Needs" activity sheet for each member; writing materials.

Description:

A. The group leader tells short story to illustrate how five basic human needs might have been met by prehistoric man.
B. Each participant is given the "Human Needs" activity sheet. The leader explains the example shown on the activity sheet and asks if anyone has any questions.
C. Each member fills in the blank pyramid in his or her own words.
D. Members are asked to voluntarily share their answers.

Group Discussion:

- The group leader tells this story to illustrate the five basic human needs in a humorous manner: "Once upon a time, before there were cars, telephones, houses, guns, or even VCRs, there lived a man named Hukum. Hukum woke up one morning and wanted to eat. So he took his spear and went hunting for a wild boar. He chased down the boar, killed it, and brought it back to his cave. He was satisfying the first basic human need — his *Survival* need. Sitting in his cave, he felt safe from dangerous animals or the environment. This satisfied his *Security* need. Hukum wanted to share his need with others so he invited all his friends for dinner. This satisfied his *Social* needs. His friends told him that he made the best wild boar they'd ever tasted. Hukum felt good about himself which satisfied his *Self-Respect* needs. Hukum decided to collect all his favorite recipes for wild boar and wrote a cookbook which supported his *Self-Actualization* need. The book's title was 'The Wild Julia Child.' "
- The group leader should emphasize that each participant's daily behavior demonstrates the basic needs they are working on fulfilling.
- This exercise can be used with a variety of age groups at all stages of development because it can be interpreted on many levels.

Human Needs

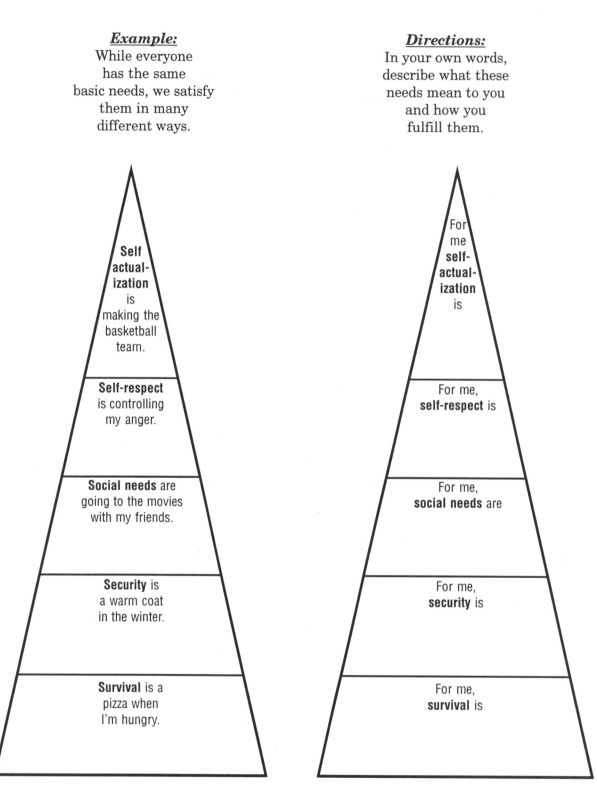

Example:
While everyone
has the same
basic needs, we satisfy
them in many
different ways.

Directions:
In your own words,
describe what these
needs mean to you
and how you
fulfill them.

Self actual-ization is making the basketball team.

Self-respect is controlling my anger.

Social needs are going to the movies with my friends.

Security is a warm coat in the winter.

Survival is a pizza when I'm hungry.

For me **self-actual-ization** is

For me, **self-respect** is

For me, **social needs** are

For me, **security** is

For me, **survival** is

Backpacking Experience

Purpose:

    1. To identify the five basic human needs when put into a survival situation.

    2. To facilitate group interaction by sharing personal information.

Materials:

    One copy of the "Backpack" activity sheet for each member; writing materials; newsprint or chalkboard; paper.

Description:

    A. The group leader asks members to think about what it would be like to go on a 1-week backpacking trip by themselves. They would be responsible for planning what goes into the backpack for their own survival. Review the five basic human needs as stated in the "Human Needs" exercise (pp. 101-102).

    B. Divide the group into small groups. Instruct each group member to make a list of their personal items to be brought on the trip. When they complete their individual lists, group members look for similarities in items they listed.

    C. While handing out the activity sheets, the leader asks each group to separate items into the five categories of human needs. The leader then facilitates a discussion about the items and needs they fulfill.

Group Discussion:

- To prepare the group for this exercise, the leader can list on the board items such as dried fruit, matches, family pictures, nature guidebook, biodegradable soap, harmonica, and so on. Next to each item, the human need it fulfills is written and discussed. For example, biodegradable soap might support a self-respect need as it helps to keep the environment clean. The nature guidebook could fulfill a survival or a self-actualization need.

- The group may choose to reevaluate what need their item is fulfilling during the group discussion.

- This exercise should follow the "Human Needs" exercise (pp. 101-102), and works best with group members who are able to think abstractly as well as logically.

Backpack

Directions: Make a list of items you would take for a 1-week backpacking trip by yourself. Label each item with the need it fulfills.

Human Needs: Survival, Security, Social, Self-Respect, Self-Actualization

Backpack Items	Human Needs They Fulfill

Shadow Conversations

Purpose:

1. To gain visual appreciation of verbal and nonverbal interaction.
2. To increase awareness of the relationship between verbal expression and nonverbal or body language.

Materials:

Slide projector; large pieces of white mural paper; magic markers; tape.

Description:

A. The leader asks the group if they have ever seen their shadow against a building or on a sidewalk, or when walking with a friend if they have seen both shadow figures together. The leader explains that what they will be doing in this exercise is making shadows of themselves in conversation with others.

B. The slide projector is turned on and pointed toward a large piece of white paper taped on a wall. The group members are asked to pair up and decide on a conversation involving one verbal exchange. An example may be given with one person saying, "Hey, why didn't you call me last night?" The response could be, "I'm sorry, but I really forgot." Members are encouraged to use a variety of feelings such as joy, sadness, surprise, anger, and so on.

C. Each pair takes turns standing in front of the paper while holding the appropriate posture that reflects the conversation. The leader outlines the shadows, and the conversation taking place is written over the figures (see illustration on next page).

D. When completed, the shadow conversations are put up around the room for display and discussion.

Group Discussion:

- Members describe the body language that expresses their conversation written above their shadows. Members comment on whether they think the body language portrays the conversation accurately, and why or why not.
- Group members discuss how body language can be interpreted and how this knowledge can be helpful in realizing the feelings of others during an interaction.
- This exercise can be a lot of fun and is effective with a variety of groups during all stages of group development.

Shadow Conversations

Body Talk

Purpose:

1. To identify different feelings through observing nonverbal communication.
2. To increase awareness of personal and other group members' feelings and their expression.

Materials:

3" x 5" index cards; newsprint or blackboard; markers; "Body Talk" activity sheet for each member.

Description:

A. A list of the "Feeling Words" (pp. 113-115) are written on the board, and a discussion is initiated about the different feelings and their meaning.
B. The group leader writes each of the 10 words from the "Feeling Word List" (pp. 113-115) on three index cards for a total of 30 cards.
C. Group members sit in a circle and are given a card until everyone has the same number of cards. Extra cards are not used. The leader asks each participant to read the feeling word on their cards and think of how they would "act out" each emotion without talking. To prepare the group for this exercise, the leader may demonstrate one of the feeling words.
D. The leader asks each participant to take a turn acting out one feeling. Each observing group member then picks a card from their hand that they think matches the feeling being acted out. Members who correctly match the feeling are identified by the actor, and then give their card to the group leader. This process is repeated until one or more participants "win" by running out of cards. Everyone then discusses the results and the activity sheet.

Group Discussion:

- The leader helps members explore the meaning of each feeling by asking them to think of a time they might have felt that way and why. Participants should not feel any pressure to be included in the exercise, and should be reassured that it is their choice to do so. The purpose for having "winners" in this exercise is to create focus and attention with observing group members.
- The leader asks members why it is important to be more aware of one's own as well as others' body language and how it can assist in congruent communication (e.g., if someone is feeling sad verses angry, one's reaction would change accordingly). A "Feeling Word List" can be derived from the "Feeling Connection" activity sheet (see pp. 113-115).
- Each member is given a copy of the "Body Talk" activity sheet, and the importance of observing nonverbal communication is discussed. This activity could be brought home and filled out for next group.
- This exercise can benefit all ages and group types.

Body Talk

Directions: Keep a record of ways people, both yourself and others, try to communicate their feelings nonverbally (without saying anything). Note the reaction that the nonverbal communication got from others or observers, and decide if the reaction was in line with the nonverbal communication.

Nonverbal Communication	Reaction of Observer	Thoughts on Reaction
Example: hands on hips, eyebrows scrunched together.	*Example:* "What's wrong?"	*Example:* Nonverbal communication was anger. I agree.

Self-Talk

Purpose:

1. To understand what self-talk is and how it directs one's thoughts and behaviors.
2. To identify one's positive and negative patterns of self-talk.
3. To provide an opportunity for choosing positive self-talk.

Materials:

Paper; writing materials.

Description:

A. The leader explores with the group differences between positive and negative self-talk and the possible effects on one's thoughts and behaviors. The leader explains that most people carry on a silent conversation with themselves during much of the day, and this is called "Self-Talk." It's also explained that these internal dialogues can actually direct someone's thoughts and behaviors. If one thinks, "I know I can do that job," they'll be more willing to apply and have a much better chance of success. If one says to oneself, "I'll never get hired for that job," they'll probably not even apply, guaranteeing that they won't get the job.

B. While handing out sheets of paper, the leader tells the members to draw three columns on the sheet. In the first column, they are instructed to write several things they would like to happen (e.g., "I'd like to lose 10 pounds"; "I'd like to have my own pet").

C. Members are asked to close their eyes and listen to how they respond to each item. Then they write their "self-talk" in the second column (e.g., "I can't do it"; "I'll go to the pet store today and look at the bunnies").

D. In the third column each member writes down a thought which is the *opposite* of the one in column two (e.g., "I can lose 10 pounds"; "I don't know how to take care of a pet"). (See illustration on p. 110 for example.)

Group Discussion:

- Participants look over their lists. If column two is more positive than column three, the leader explains that they are on their way to thinking positively because their first thought was the positive one and the one that will likely influence their behaviors. If column two is more negative, they are encouraged to look at column three for a more helpful, healthier response.
- Group members can discuss their "scripts" of self-talk in a large group or divided into pairs.
- This exercise is most effective with groups that are beyond the early stage of development.

Self-Talk

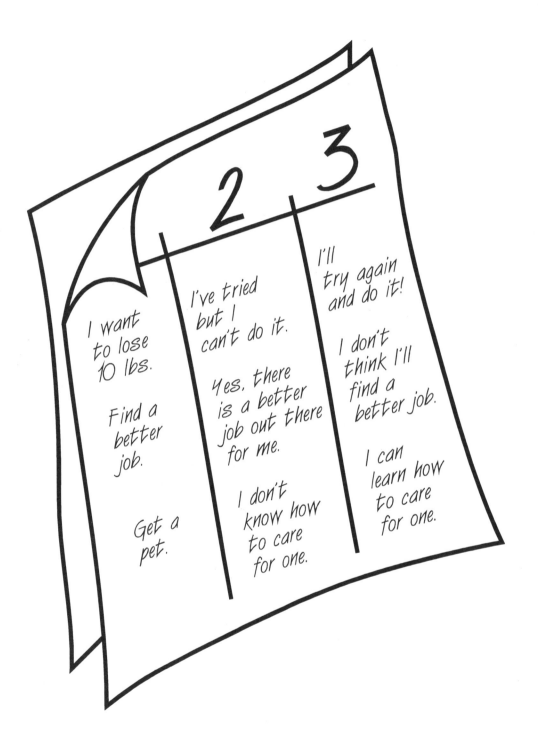

Wisdom Fantasy

Purpose:

1. To identify behaviors that support a sense of well-being.
2. To encourage group members to take responsibility for personal growth.
3. To promote a trust in oneself, or wisdom.

Materials:

Drawing paper; markers; crayons; writing materials.

Description:

A. The group leader defines wisdom as being able to apply acquired knowledge in a correct way. A person who can accomplish this is wise.
B. The group is asked to be seated or to lie on the floor in a circle. The leader instructs participants to take a few deep breaths and to close their eyes while listening to an imaginary story.
C. The leader then tells the following story: "Picture yourself in a large open meadow with green trees, yellow, white, and purple flowers, and light green grass. You can smell the sweet aroma of the flowers. Now look toward a small mountain beyond the meadow and begin slowly walking up the mountain until you reach the top. The air is clean and refreshing to breathe. At the top you see a wise person sitting peacefully. You carefully approach this person and sit quietly in front of him or her. After a few minutes you ask the wise person this question: 'What do I need to do to feel good about myself?' " (Pause for a few minutes.)
D. The leader tells the participants that when they have heard the answer, they should walk back down the mountain and come back into the room, slowly opening their eyes. The leader then asks the members to draw or write down the answer they were given.
E. The group members then discuss their answers in small groups of three or four.
F. *Variation:* As a follow-up exercise, the group leader notes that "It has been stated that one picture is worth a thousand words." Group members are then asked to draw pictures (or imagine pictures) that illustrate what they have said. For example, if a member says, "I need to feel confident," these words can be reinforced by having the member create a picture illustrating the confident person they want to be. The leader can show all group members how they can use this technique to remind themselves of how pictures and images can reinforce positive feelings. This technique can be used in each group session to develop positive images and feelings.

Group Discussion:

- Each group shares its illustrations or words describing the answers to their question. The leader explores with the different groups the feelings they had listening to the wise person and if the answer given seems useful. Additionally, they discuss their feelings around sharing these answers with the group.
- The leader asks members to think about and discuss how these answers will help them to feel better about themselves, and if these are new answers.
- I have observed that members with low self-esteem can especially benefit from this exercise but might need encouragement to trust that "inner voice" that gives them good advice.
- This exercise works best with groups whose members are insightful and capable of abstract reasoning.

The Feelings Connection

Purpose:

1. To develop a vocabulary of feeling words.
2. To increase an understanding of how feelings can affect interactions with other members.

Materials:

One copy of "Feelings Connection" activity sheet for each member; writing materials.

Description:

A. The leader asks members if they feel uncomfortable talking about their feelings. They are told that many people of all ages often have a difficult time talking about how they feel and that this exercise will help them to feel more comfortable about expressing feelings.

B. As the group is given a copy of the activity sheet, it is explained that to assist them with identifying different feelings, the activity will divide feelings into two categories - *Upset* and *Upbeat*.

C. After completing the activity sheet, members are asked to give papers to the leader, who then redistributes them to other members. Participants who want to remain anonymous should not write their names on the activity sheet.

D. Sentences are read aloud and discussed.

Group Discussion:

- Each member reads a sentence aloud and discusses its meaning. If a feeling word is one that is difficult to understand, the leader defines it in another sentence.
- Often, the discussion continues further because members want to explore the experiences stated in their sentences.
- This exercise is effective with a variety of groups at any stage of development.

Feelings Connection

Directions: For each feeling word, write a sentence describing a situation in which you experienced this feeling. For example:

Feeling Word: **worried**
Sentence: I was **worried** last night because it was late and Tom didn't return.

Upset Feelings

1. angry

   _____

   _____

2. anxious

   _____

   _____

3. bored

   _____

   _____

4. confused

   _____

   _____

5. disappointed

   _____

   _____

6. disrespected

   _____

   _____

7. embarrassed

   _____

   _____

8. frightened

   _____

   _____

Feelings Connection

Directions: For each feeling word, write a sentence describing a situation in which you experienced this feeling.

Upbeat Feelings

1. accepted

_____

_____

2. appreciated

_____

_____

3. better

_____

_____

4. capable

_____

_____

5. comfortable

_____

_____

6. confident

_____

_____

7. joyful

_____

_____

8. excited

_____

_____

Drawing Emotions

Purpose:

1. To increase understanding of one's emotions in a nonthreatening way.
2. To create a healthy expression of one's emotions.
3. To promote a group cohesiveness around creative expression of feelings.

Materials:

Drawing paper; markers; crayons; tempera paint; brushes.

Description:

A. The leader begins this exercise by asking the group if they've ever heard expressions such as "He's so angry, he sees red!" or "I'm feeling blue" or "She's such a warm person." A short discussion that focuses on how people often express emotions through colors and temperatures is facilitated by the leader.

B. While handing out materials, the leader explains that in this exercise they are going to express an emotion or feeling through spontaneous drawings. Participants can be divided into small groups or work individually.

C. The group leader calls out a feeling word and asks participants to use any of the art materials available to express the feeling with a realistic or abstract drawing. Participants are given 3 to 5 minutes per drawing, and each drawing should be labeled with the corresponding feeling.

D. After completing three or four drawings, the group discusses and displays their artwork.

Group Discussion:

- Feeling words that the leader calls out can include: scared, curious, lonely, bored, joyful, connected, suspicious, modest, confident, tired, nervous, and healthy. The leader should use a balance of words that might evoke positive or negative feelings. Participants often need encouragement to express themselves in a spontaneous and abstract manner.

- The leader should emphasize the possible benefits of permitting themselves to create drawings without feeling judged on their artistic value or correctness. Some possible benefits can include an increased sense of confidence in how to identify feelings, a feeling of wholeness in self, and release of stress.

- Employing the creative process as a means of personal and artistic growth in a nonthreatening way can be effective with groups in all stages of development.

The Empty Chair*

Purpose:

1. To clarify feelings, behaviors, and their consequences.
2. To facilitate a process of conflict resolution and personal responsibility for one's behavior.
3. To encourage empathy through identification with the feelings of others.

Materials:

Two chairs.

Description:

A. The leader demonstrates this exercise by sitting in one chair which faces the other empty chair. An explanation of a problem is given such as: "My friend borrowed my car, and when she returned it I noticed a small dent in the fender. I felt angry, but I never said anything to her at the time."
B. The leader begins having an imagined dialogue with the friend.

> *Model Example:*
>
> ***Leader:*** Eden, it seems that you hit something with my car but never told me, and I feel angry about it.
> ***Leader:*** (now change chairs to be ***Eden*** and say what she might say) Well, I didn't realize it happened, I really didn't.
> ***Leader:*** (changing chairs again) Well, if you say so I'll believe you.
> ***Leader:*** (as ***Eden***) Well, I feel bad about this. How about I help pay for the damage?
> ***Leader:*** (as himself or herself) Sure, that sounds fair.

C. Ask for a volunteer who has had an unresolved problem with another person and would like to try to imagine resolving it. Discuss results with group.

Group Discussion:

- In the beginning of this exercise, the leader explains how it is not uncommon for people to have feelings and thoughts about someone that are kept inside because of difficulty in communicating to them directly. An age-appropriate example should be given. Members are encouraged to give their own examples.
- When the group is discussing the exercise, these questions should be asked: How did it feel talking to an imaginary person? Was it helpful? Why or why not?
- This exercise can be an integral part of your group in processing conflicts. Two chairs can always be ready for use by group members needing to deal with unresolved conflicts. I have found that after using this technique, the individual often feels better prepared to communicate to the other person.

---

*This technique was originally developed by Fritz Perls, PhD.

Changing My Communication

Purpose:

1. To describe appropriate ways of expressing feelings.
2. To increase awareness of appropriate and inappropriate ways of communicating feelings.

Materials:

One copy of "Changing My Communication" activity sheet for each member; writing materials; chalkboard or newsprint.

Description:

A. The leader writes the heading "Angry" on the chalkboard and asks, "Who can tell me one way that you express yourself when you are angry?" After eliciting several responses, the leader asks if these are the best possible ways to respond when angry. The responses are written in column number one.
B. Group members are asked to think of some alternative positive ways of handling anger. These responses are written in a second column.
C. Members are given the activity sheet "Changing My Communication" and are asked to complete the sentences.
D. When members have completed the sheets, volunteers are asked to share their ideas concerning appropriate ways to express each feeling.

Group Discussion:

- When discussing alternative positive ways of handling anger, the leader can facilitate discussion by asking these questions:

  ▷ How does it feel when you behave in the ways we listed in the second column?
  ▷ How do you think people around you feel when you express yourself as stated in the first column? Second column?

- This exercise can be helpful in assisting emotionally immature group members to organize their thoughts and approach effective communication in a structured and nonthreatening manner. It can be used effectively with a variety of groups and ages.

Changing My Communication

Directions: Describe in writing the things you usually do and say to express these feelings listed below. Then see if you can change your communication by writing a *more positive way* to express yourself in the second column.

When I am angry, I usually express myself by:

_____

_____

_____

A more *positive* way to express my anger would

be to: _____

_____

_____

When I am sad, I usually express myself by:

_____

_____

_____

A more *positive* way to express my sadness

would be to: _____

_____

_____

When I am happy, I usually express myself

by: _____

_____

_____

A more *positive* way to express my happiness

would be to: _____

_____

_____

When I am frustrated, I usually express my-

self by: _____

_____

_____

A more *positive* way to express my frustra-

tion would be to: _____

_____

_____

When I am bored, I usually express myself by:

_____

_____

_____

A more *positive* way to express my boredom

would be to: _____

_____

_____

Talk and Listen

Purpose:

1. To develop listening and speaking skills.
2. To increase socialization skills.
3. To facilitate group interaction by sharing personal information.

Materials:

Small bell or cooking timer.

Description:

A. The leader asks group members to sit in pairs, facing their partners. Each partner will take turns being a "listener" and then a "speaker."
B. Each partner will be given 3 minutes each to either listen or talk about the topic being discussed.
C. The group leader will ring the bell after 3 minutes, letting each pair finish their sentences or thoughts before changing roles to either a "listener" or "speaker." After they both have taken turns, members form a large group and share information one at a time.

Group Discussion:

- The group leader explains to the participants that in order for two people to enjoy and encourage each other to work, socialize, or solve problems together, they need to be able to communicate effectively. In communication there is always a speaker and a listener. The leader reminds group participants to speak clearly and to the point and to try and listen without interrupting or thinking about something else while listening.
- When each pair shares information discussed with large groups, the leader explains that the person listening will report what the speaker was saying, so it's important to really listen.
- List of possible topics: "What I Did Last Night"; "A Problem I Need to Solve"; "Something I'd Like to Do Better"; "A Time I Really Enjoyed Myself."
- This exercise can be used with a variety of groups in any stage of development.

Listening on Purpose

Purpose:

1. To develop careful listening skills.
2. To describe the importance of good listening to friendships, family, and relationships.

Materials:

Audiocassette recorder and blank tape; chalkboard or newsprint.

Description:

A. The group leader asks participants to sit in pairs and have a short discussion about a favorite TV program.
B. While the members are talking, the leader inconspicuously moves around the room and tapes some of their comments in casual conversation.
C. The leader writes "Listen!" on the chalkboard in large letters and asks group members to stop talking and listen for a few moments to the tape recorder. The leader then asks, "What is special about the way a tape recorder listens?"
D. The facilitator helps the group recognize that a tape recorder is very accurate and hears every word just the way it's said.
E. Members sit in pairs and decide who will play the part of the tape recorder first. Have the "tape recorders" raise their hands. The leader announces this topic to be discussed: "What I'd like to do on my birthday." Tell the speakers to start talking and the "tape recorders" to start recording.
F. After 1 minute of talking, the leader gives the next instruction: *Now the "tape recorders" will have 1 minute to repeat what they heard, while the speakers listen.*
G. Have the members switch roles and repeat the entire process using the same topic.

Group Discussion:

- After the first 1 minute of discussion, the members are asked these questions:

  ▷ What was it like to listen like a tape recorder?
  ▷ Speakers, how well did your "tape recorder" (listener) work?
  ▷ What was it like to be listened to so well?

- Leaving 10 minutes at the end of the exercise, members are asked to discuss one or more of the following questions:

  ▷ Why is it important to listen carefully when someone is talking?
  ▷ Why is it important to listen to your parents? Your teacher? Your friends?

- This exercise is effective with a variety of groups at all stages of development.

Be Cool and Cool Off

Purpose:

1. To provide an understanding of the use of effective, nonaggressive communication.
2. To compare "I" and "You" messages, and be able to describe their differences.
3. To identify the three parts of an "I" message and practice their formation.

Materials:

One copy of the "Be Cool and Cool Off" activity sheet for each member; chalkboard or newsprint; markers; writing materials (optional videotaping equipment*).

Description:

A. The leader writes on the board; "I message" and "You message" and explains that "I messages" are used when you have a problem that needs to be expressed to someone else and "You messages" are ones that often place blame and verbally attack another person.
B. The group leader checks for group understanding by asking which of the two types of statements might lead to someone feeling attacked and needing to defend themselves. Why?
C. While handing out activity sheets, the leader asks each member to listen while the first example is read aloud. Members are then asked to complete the exercise sheets while the leader checks for understanding.
D. Members are asked to pair up and choose one example each of "I" and "You" messages from their exercise sheets. Volunteers are then asked to role-play their examples for the group by standing up and reading their examples aloud.
E. *Variation:* If group members feel comfortable, videotaping role-plays and viewing them with discussions can act as added reinforcement to participating and developing new skills.

Group Discussion:

- The group's discussion first centers on the fact that miscommunication is the largest part of any conflict. The group leader points out the importance of expressing one's feelings without attacking or blaming the other person first.
- The leader points out to the participants that using "I messages" may feel awkward at first, but with practice they will feel a greater sense of confidence in effectively communicating their feelings to others. The example may be used of how playing an instrument or learning a new sport might have felt awkward at first but with practice became more natural and enjoyable.
- This exercise should follow Exercise #56 (pp. 121-122) and Exercise #58 (p. 125) and can be used with a variety of groups and ages.

Be Cool and Cool Off

Directions: Try using "I" statements rather than "You" statements when you are angry and when you want to communicate your feelings. Instead of talking about the other person by attacking or blaming them ("You" statements), talk about your *feelings and needs* ("I" statements). "You" statements tend to blame the other person and lead to their feeling attacked and needing to defend themselves.

Here is an example of how a "You" statement can be changed to an assertive "I" statement.

"<u>You</u> make fun of my mother again and you're gonna be real sorry."

could be changed to:

"<u>I feel</u> upset <u>when you</u> make fun of my mother <u>because</u> I thought you were my friend."

YOUR TURN

Directions: Write down an example of a "You" statement and an "I" statement *alternative*.

Problem: Your friends said they would call you about something important and forgot.

"You" statement: _____

_____

"I" statement: _____

_____

Problem: A group member makes fun of what you're wearing.

"You" statement: _____

_____

"I" statement: _____

_____

Problem: A group member makes a joke about something you did but you don't find it funny.

"You" statement: _____

_____

"I" statement: _____

_____

Problem: (Your choice)

"You" statement: _____

_____

"I" statement: _____

_____

Problem: (Your choice)

"You" statement: _____

_____

"I" statement: _____

_____

Problem: (Your choice)

"You" statement: _____

_____

"I" statement: _____

_____

Please visit us online at:

http://www.prpress.com

This website contains:

- ✓ Descriptions of all of our titles with
  - • complete tables of contents
  - • reviews of our books
  - • author biographies
- ✓ Online ordering
- ✓ Online queries and requests for catalogs
- ✓ Information on our home-study continuing education programs
- ✓ Our publishing guidelines
- ✓ The history of our company

. . . . and much, much more!

Catalog Request

For our latest catalog and ordering information, please write, call, fax, or e-mail the following information:

Name: _____
PLEASE PRINT CLEARLY

Address (Company name if business address): _____

Address: _____

City/State/Zip: _____ Country: _____

Phone Number: _____

I am a (check one):

❑ Psychologist ❑ School Psychologist
❑ Clinical Social Worker ❑ Psychiatrist
❑ Marriage and Family Therapist ❑ Other: _____
❑ Mental Health Counselor

Please send this form to: Professional Resource Press, PO Box 15560, Sarasota, FL 34277-1560.
You can also contact us by phone (1-800-443-3364), FAX (1-941-343-9201),
or e-mail (orders@prpress.com).

Please visit us online at:

http://www.prpress.com

This website contains:

✓ Descriptions of all of our titles with
- • complete tables of contents
- • reviews of our books
- • author biographies
✓ Online ordering
✓ Online queries and requests for catalogs
✓ Information on our home-study continuing education programs
✓ Our publishing guidelines
✓ The history of our company

. . . . and much, much more!

- -

Catalog Request

For our latest catalog and ordering information, please write, call, fax, or e-mail the following information:

Name: _____
PLEASE PRINT CLEARLY

Address (Company name if business address): _____

Address: _____

City/State/Zip: _____ Country: _____

Phone Number: _____

I am a (check one):

❑ Psychologist ❑ School Psychologist
❑ Clinical Social Worker ❑ Psychiatrist
❑ Marriage and Family Therapist ❑ Other: _____
❑ Mental Health Counselor

Please send this form to: Professional Resource Press, PO Box 15560, Sarasota, FL 34277-1560.
You can also contact us by phone (1-800-443-3364), FAX (1-941-343-9201),
or e-mail (orders@prpress.com).